The Crochet Handbook and Stitch Guide

The Crochet Handbook and Stitch Guide

Essential crochet techniques and stitch patterns
to improve your skills

Edited by Ruth Patrick

CHARTWELL
BOOKS, INC.

A QUARTO BOOK

Published in 2009 by
Chartwell Books, Inc.
A division of Book Sales, Inc.
276 Fifth Avenue, Suite 206
New York, New York 10001
USA

Reprinted 2011 , 2012 (three times) , 2013

ISBN 13: 978-0-7858-2556-2
ISBN 10: 0-7858-2556-8
QUAR.CSG

Conceived, designed, and produced by
Quarto Publishing plc
The Old Brewery
6 Blundell Street
London N7 9BH

Senior editor: Ruth Patrick
Designer: Luise Crawford
Design assistant: Saffron Stocker
Picture researcher: Sarah Bell
Proofreader: Sally MacEachern
Indexer: Ann Barrett

Art director: Caroline Guest
Creative director: Moira Clinch
Publisher: Paul Carslake

Manufactured in Singapore by Pica Digital
   International Pte Ltd.
Printed in China by Midas Printing
   International Ltd.

Contents

Introduction 6

Introduction

Crochet is one of the easiest crafts to take
up because you need very little initial
equipment; just a ball of yarn and a crochet
hook. All the stitches are based on the
simple action of wrapping yarn around
a hook and hooking or drawing it through
a loop. The number of times the yarn is
wrapped, and when, can vary, as can the
number of loops, but, unlike knitting,
after each stitch there remains only one
loop. The simplicity of this single loop
at the end of a stitch is exactly what makes
it an exciting craft because the direction
and position of the next stitch can change
instantly and so the number of possible
combinations appears almost endless.
As you may let your mind wander, so it
is possible to let your hook wander as the
muse takes you at that moment.

Equipment

This is not a craft that needs a huge investment, but like many crafts it is possible to accumulate a selection of hooks and equipment and then favor only a few. This is encouraged by the fact that most of the equipment is relatively inexpensive and this in turn can serve a purpose if you tend to have several projects on the go at any one time. Keeping a set of basic tools with each project can be helpful. For hook sizes see page 176.

Crochet hooks

Crochet hooks are available in a wide range of sizes, shapes, and materials. The most common sorts of hooks used for working with the types of yarn covered in this book are made from aluminum or plastic. Small sizes of steel hooks are also made for working crochet with very fine cotton yarns. (This type of fine work is known as thread crochet.) Some brands of aluminum and steel hooks have plastic handles to give a better grip (often called "soft touch" handles) and make the work easier on the fingers. Hand-made wooden and horn hooks are also available, many featuring decorative handles.

There appears to be no standardization of hook sizing between manufacturers. The points and throats of different brands of hooks often vary in shape which affects the size of stitch they produce.

Hook sizes are quoted differently in the United States and Europe and some brands of hooks are labeled with more than one type of numbering. Choosing a hook is largely a matter of personal

Anatomy of the crochet hook

Point

Throat

Thumb rest

Shank

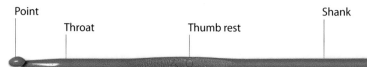

preference and will depend on various factors such as hand size, finger length, weight of hook, and whether you like the feel of aluminum or plastic in your hand.

The hook sizes quoted in pattern instructions are a very useful guide, but you may find that you need to use smaller or larger hook sizes, depending on the brand, to achieve the correct gauge for a pattern. The most important thing to consider when choosing a hook is how it feels in your hand and the ease with which it works with your yarn. When you have found your perfect brand of hook, it's useful to buy a range of several different sizes. Store your hooks in a clean container—you can buy a fabric roll with loops to secure the hooks, or use a zippered pouch such as a cosmetic bag.

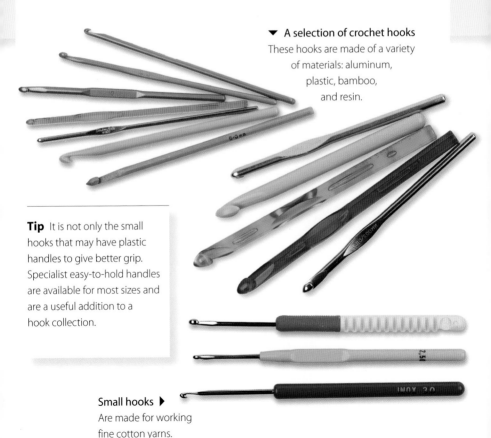

▼ A selection of crochet hooks
These hooks are made of a variety of materials: aluminum, plastic, bamboo, and resin.

Tip It is not only the small hooks that may have plastic handles to give better grip. Specialist easy-to-hold handles are available for most sizes and are a useful addition to a hook collection.

Small hooks ▶
Are made for working fine cotton yarns.

Additional equipment

Working a crochet project can be divided into two stages: crocheting and finishing. The crocheting stage is often far more portable and can be done with a little less concentration as you go about your day. The final finishing of a piece is best done quietly, at home, with very good light—so many of the items for this stage are best kept safely at home. Some specialist equipment is required for Tunisian, broomstick, and hairpin crochet: Tunisian crochet requires a specialist hook; broomstick crochet a piece of dowel or broomstick; hairpin crochet a steel U-shaped frame.

Traveling working kit

It is helpful to keep this selection with the project whether it is by your chair or in a small bag that you carry round with you. A word of caution however, plastic does not make the best material for a project bag because the static it creates may attract dust.

Sharp scissors

Choose a small, pointed pair to cut yarn and trim off yarn ends. If you're traveling on an airplane, leave scissors at home.

Tape measure

Choose one that shows both inches and centimeters on the same side and replace when it becomes worn as this means it will probably have stretched and become inaccurate. For the traveling bag, a tape measure that self-spools is useful.

Tapestry
needles

Tape measure

Sharp scissors

Tapestry needles

Tapestry needles have blunt points and long eyes and are normally used for counted thread embroidery. They come in a range of sizes and are used for weaving in yarn ends and for sewing pieces of crochet together. Very large blunt-pointed needles are often labeled as "yarn needles."

Markers

Split rings or shaped loops made from brightly colored plastic can be slipped onto your crochet to mark a place on a pattern, to indicate the beginning row of a repeat, and to help with counting the stitches on the foundation chain.

Row counter

A knitter's row counter will help you keep track of the number of rows you have worked, or you may prefer to use a notebook and pencil.

Waste yarn

For more long-term reference, a length of waste yarn can be used to mark stitches and rows.

Notebook

Always keep notes as you work. It is good practice and, whatever you may think at the time, one's memory is not always the most reliable—even if only a short time has elapsed.

Home and finishing working kit

Your home kit should include some of the equipment in your travel kit, and in addition the following are helpful.

Ruler

A 12 in. (30 cm) metal or plastic ruler is useful for measuring gauge swatches.

Pins

Glass-headed rustproof pins are the best type to use for blocking (pages 98–99).

Sewing needles

Sewing needles with sharp points for applying crochet braid, edging, or borders to fabric.

Quilters' long pins

Quilters' long pins with fancy heads are useful when pinning pieces of crochet together as the heads are easy to see and won't slip through the crochet fabric.

Pins

Quilters' long pins

Yarns

Yarns for crochet come in a wide variety of materials, weights, colors, and price ranges and it's important to choose the right yarn to suit your project. Yarns are usually made by spinning different types of fibers together. The fibers may be natural materials obtained from animals or plants, for example wool or cotton, or they can be man-made fibers such as nylon or acrylic. For more information on yarn weights see page 178.

Yarns may be made from one fiber or combine a mixture of two or three different ones in varying proportions. Several fine strands of yarn (called "plies") are often twisted together to make thicker weights of yarn. Novelty yarns such as tweeds and other textured yarns combine several strands of differing weights and textures twisted together. Metallics and ribbon yarns are constructed by knitting very fine yarn into tubes and giving them a rounded or flattened appearance.

Yarn is sold by weight, rather than by length, although the packaging of many yarns now includes length per ball as well as other information. It is usually packaged into balls, although some yarns may come in the form of hanks or skeins which need to be wound by hand into balls before you can begin to crochet. The most common ball size is 1¾ oz (50 g) and the length of yarn in the ball will vary depending on thickness and fiber content.

Animal fibers

Wool is the most commonly used natural fiber because it is soft, warm to wear, relatively inexpensive, and keeps its shape well. Woolen yarns are spun from the shorn fleeces of

Silk and cotton mix

Silk

sheep—other, more expensive animal fibers include mohair and cashmere (from goats) and angora (from angora rabbits), and are shorn or combed from the animal before being spun into yarn. Woolen yarns (or blended yarns with a high proportion of wool) feel nice to crochet with as they have a certain amount of stretch, making it easy to push the point of the hook into each stitch. Some yarns made from pure wool have to be laundered carefully by hand, although many are now treated to make them machine washable. Silk, spun from the unwound cocoons of the silkworm, is also a natural product. Silk yarn—like wool—is a good insulator, and has a delightful luster, although it has less resilience and is much more expensive.

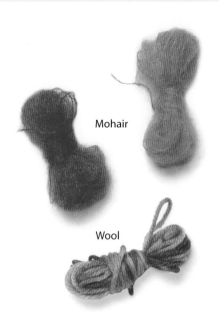

Mohair

Wool

Synthetic fibers

Acrylic, nylon, polyester, and other synthetic fibers are manufactured from coal and petroleum products and are often made to resemble natural fibers. Yarns made wholly from synthetic fibers are usually less expensive, and although they are stable, machine washable, and don't shrink, they can lose their shape when heat is applied. The best solution is to choose a yarn where a small or equal proportion of synthetic fibers has been combined with a natural fiber such as wool or cotton.

Vegetable products

Both cotton and linen are derived from plants and are popular choices for summer garments as well as home furnishings. Crochet fabric made from cotton is durable and cool to wear, but pure cotton may lack resilience and is often blended with other fibers. Pure cotton and linen yarns are also rather prone to shrinkage. Rayon (viscose), a plant-based, man-made material, is soft and slightly shiny, and because it lacks elasticity it is usually combined with other fibers.

14 Basic Crochet

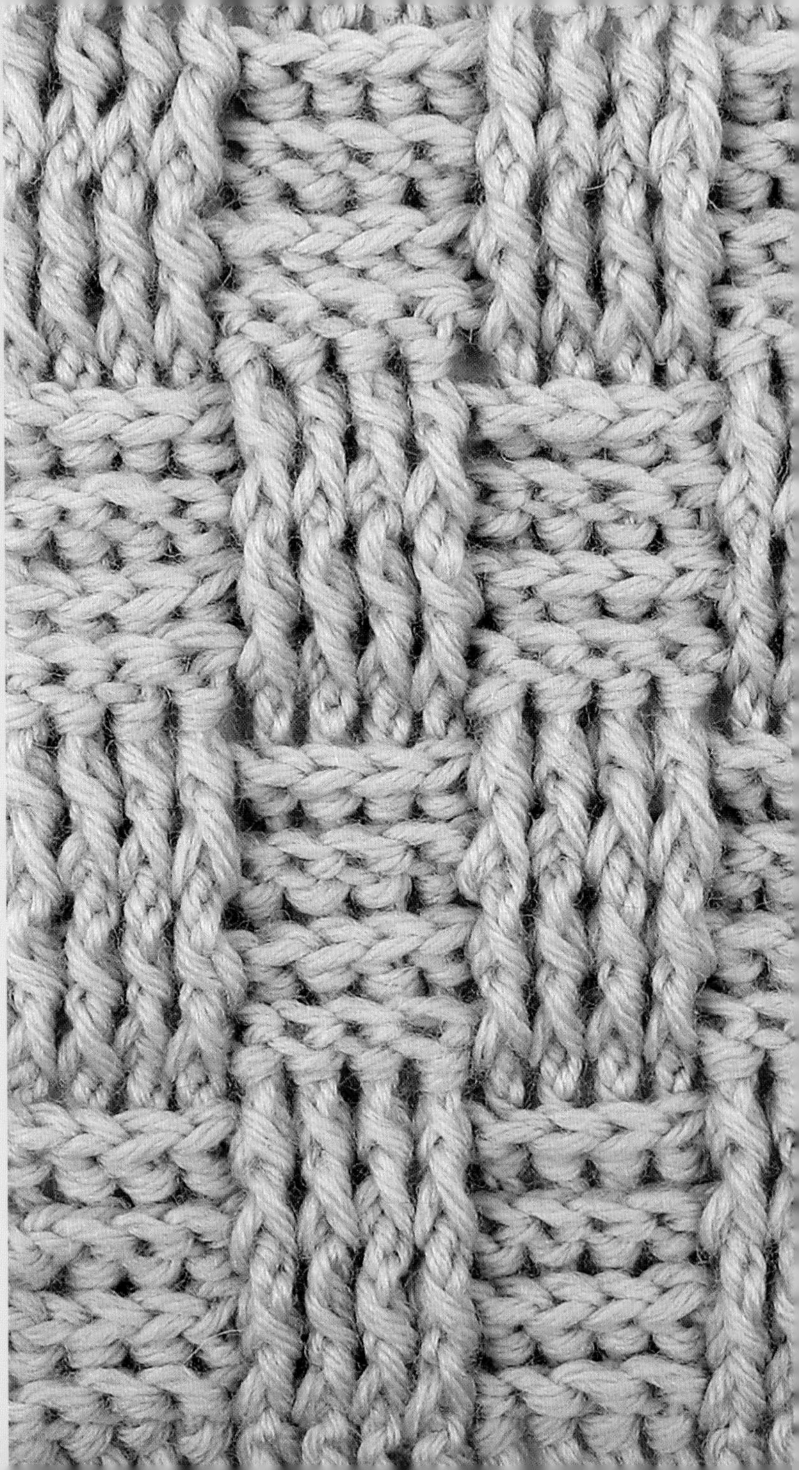

Basic Crochet

Getting started

To begin practicing crochet, choose a smooth woolen yarn of double knitting or sport weight and a compatible hook size of E–G (3.5–4.5 mm). Woolen yarn has a certain amount of "give" and is very easy to work with when you're a beginner. You can find more information on hooks and yarns on pages 8–13. If you are left-handed you may want to view the following pages with the aid of a mirror.

Holding the hook

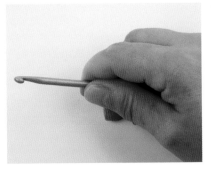

This is the most widely used way of holding the hook—as if it were a pen. Center the tips of your right thumb and forefinger over the flat section of the hook.

An alternative way is to grasp the flat section of the hook between your right thumb and forefinger as if you were holding a knife.

Holding the yarn

To control the yarn supply, loop the short end of the yarn over your left forefinger and take the yarn coming from the ball loosely round the little finger on the same hand to gauge it. Use your middle finger to help hold the work as you crochet.

A variation on this position is to loop the yarn around the back of the ring finger. This also leaves the middle finger free to hold the work. The yarn is gauged round the ring finger of the left hand.

Making a slip knot

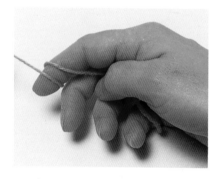

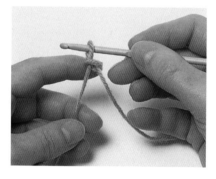

1 With about 6 in. (15 cm) of the end of the yarn at the left, loop the yarn round your right forefinger. Carefully slip the loop off your finger. Holding the loop in your right hand, push a loop of the short end through the first loop.

2 Insert the hook into the second loop. Gently pull the short end of the yarn to tighten the loop round the hook and complete the slip knot.

Chain and slip stitches

The foundation chain is the equivalent of casting on in knitting, and it's important to make sure that you have made the required number of chains for the pattern you are going to work. The front of the chain looks like a series of V shapes or little hearts, while the back of the chain forms a distinctive "bump" of yarn behind each V shape. You can count the stitches on either the front or back of the chain, whichever you find easier.

Working a chain

1 Holding the hook with the slip knot in your right hand and the yarn in your left, wrap the yarn over the hook. This is known as yarn over or yarn over hook.

Tip When working a long foundation chain, slip a ring marker into the chain to mark every 20 or 30 stitches. This will make it easier to count the chain stitches.

2 Draw the yarn through to make a new loop and complete the first chain stitch. Repeat this step, drawing a new loop of yarn through the loop on the hook until the chain is the required length. Move up the thumb and forefinger that are grasping the chain after every few stitches to keep the gauge even.

Working into a foundation chain

ch

Into the top loop Holding the chain with the front facing you, insert the hook into the top loop of each chain. Although this gives rather a loose edge to a piece of crochet, it's ideal when an edge finish (pages 109–111) is to be worked in this way.

Into the back bump To make a stronger, neater edge which can stand alone (without an edge finish being needed), turn the chain so the back of it is facing you. Work the first row of stitches of your pattern, inserting the hook into the "bump" at the back of each chain stitch.

Slip stitch (sl st)

Slip stitch is rarely used to create a crochet fabric on its own—it can almost be described as a chain stitch through a loop or loops. Slip stitch is normally used to join rounds of crochet and to move the hook and yarn across a group of existing stitches. To work a slip stitch into the foundation chain, insert the hook from front to back under the top loop of the second chain from the hook. Wrap the yarn over the hook and draw it through both the chain and the loop on the hook. One loop remains on the hook and one slip stitch has been worked.

sl st

+ Single crochet (sc)

Single crochet is the shortest stitch in crochet after the slip stitch. It produces a dense fabric and has poor drape even when worked through just one loop (see page 29). However, it is very hard wearing and, when it is worked as a firm fabric, has very little stretch. This means it is often used to neaten the edges of both crocheted and knitted fabrics and is ideal for projects such as cushions and bags. Commonly represented in charts as a cross.

Working a single crochet stitch (sc)

1 To work a row of single crochet stitches into the foundation chain, insert the hook from front to back under the top loop of the second chain from the hook. Wrap the yarn over the hook and draw it through the first loop, leaving two loops on the hook.

2 To complete the stitch, wrap the yarn over the hook and draw it through both loops on the hook. Continue in this way along the row, working one single crochet stitch into each chain.

Working a single crochet fabric

At the end of the row, turn and work one chain for the turning chain. (This chain does not count as a stitch.) Insert the hook from front to back under both loops of the first single crochet at the beginning of the row. Work a single crochet stitch into each stitch of the previous row, being careful to work the final single crochet stitch into the last stitch of the row below, but not into the turning chain.

Extended single crochet

To work an extended single crochet stitch, insert the hook, from front to back, in the required location. Wrap the yarn over the hook and draw it through; two loops on the hook. Wrap the yarn over the hook and draw it through one loop; again two loops on the hook. Wrap the yarn over the hook and draw it through both loops on the hook.

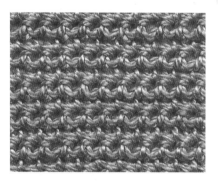

▲ Single crochet fabric

A relatively smooth fabric, it is often used for Jacquard work because its close fabric easily hides any floats on the reverse. Its sturdy fabric is also popular for dense beading.

Tip It is easy with single crochet to achieve an equal stitch and row gauge for a given distance—a square stitch. Useful for charting color work designs.

(T) Half double crochet (hdc)

This stitch is the next up in height from single crochet (see page 20). Half double crochet is very popular as a solid fabric because it has substance but the drape is better than single crochet.
It is often used as a halfway-height stitch between the more elongated double stitch and the anchoring single crochet stitch. Commonly represented in charts as a vertical line topped with a horizontal line—a "T" shape.

Working a half double crochet stitch (hdc)

1 To work a half double crochet stitch, wrap the yarn over the hook and insert the hook from front to back into the work. (If you are at the beginning of the first row, insert hook under the top loop of the third chain from the hook.)

2 Draw the yarn through the chain, leaving three loops on the hook. Wrap the yarn over the hook and draw through all three loops on the hook. One loop remains on the hook and one half double crochet stitch has been worked. Continue along the row, working one half double crochet stitch into each chain.

Working a half double crochet fabric

T
hdc

1 At the end of the row, work two chains for the turning chain and turn. Skipping the first half double crochet stitch at the beginning of the row, wrap the yarn over the hook, insert the hook from front to back under both loops of the second stitch on the previous row, and work a half double crochet stitch into each stitch made on the previous row.

2 At the end of the row, work the last stitch into the top of the turning chain.

▲ **Half double crochet fabric**
A slightly knobbly fabric, the joy of this stitch is the speed at which it can be worked and the additional flexibility in stitch placement that the back bar provides.

The back bar

On the reverse of a half double crochet stitch, just below the two top loops, is a prominent, horizontal yarn strand. A pattern will sometimes indicate to work into this back bar which means inserting the hook from front to back under this strand of yarn. As the top loops are not worked, they remain visible on the opposite side. It creates a fabric with excellent drape and an interesting texture.

Ŧ Double crochet (dc)

This stitch is the basis of many stitch patterns from textural clusters, to fine filet lace. It has good drape and the stitch height compensates for the greater time it takes to create. Commonly represented in charts as a vertical line, bisected by a diagonal line, and topped by a horizontal line—a "T" shape with a slanted line through it. The diagonal line indicates that the yarn is wrapped around the hook once before it is inserted into the fabric.

Working a double crochet stitch (dc)

1 To work a double crochet stitch, wrap the yarn over the hook and insert the hook from front to back into the work. (If you are at the beginning of the first row, insert the hook under the top loop of the fourth chain from the hook.) Draw the yarn through the chain, leaving three loops on the hook.

2 Wrap the yarn over the hook. Draw the yarn through the first two loops on the hook. Two loops remain on the hook.

3 Wrap the yarn over the hook.

4 Draw the yarn through the two loops on the hook. One loop remains on the hook and one double crochet stitch has been worked.

Working a double crochet fabric

At the end of the row, work three chains for the turning chain and turn. Skipping the first double crochet stitch at the beginning of the row, wrap the yarn over the hook, insert the hook from front to back under both loops of the second stitch on the previous row, and work a double crochet stitch into each stitch made on the previous row. At the end of the row, work the last stitch into the top of the turning chain.

▲ Double crochet fabric

A fabric made up of double crochet stitches resembles a series of ladders laid side by side. The fabric has excellent drape but still has some strength although it does not create a dense fabric and is not hard wearing.

Treble crochet (tr)

This stitch is rarely used to create a solid fabric without the support of shorter, stronger stitches. It may be used to extend the height of a group of stitches or to lighten a post or relief stitch fabric. Commonly represented on charts as a vertical line, bisected by two diagonal lines, and topped by a horizontal line. The diagonal lines indicate that the yarn is wrapped around the hook twice before it is inserted into the fabric.

Working a treble crochet stitch (tr)

1 To work a treble (triple) crochet stitch, wrap the yarn over the hook twice. Insert the hook from front to back into the work. (If you are at the beginning of the first row, insert the hook under the top loop of the fifth chain from the hook.) Wrap the yarn over the hook and draw through, leaving four loops on the hook. Wrap the yarn over the hook.

2 Draw through two loops (three loops on the hook), wrap again, draw through two loops (two loops on the hook). Wrap again and draw through the remaining two loops. Repeat along the row. At the beginning of every row, work four turning chains and insert the hook into the second stitch of the row. At the end of every row, work the last stitch into the top of the turning chain.

Other crochet stitches

Stitches taller than a treble are seen less often in patterns but follow a similar method of construction. They are defined by the number of times that the yarn is wrapped around the hook before it is inserted into the fabric and are usually represented on charts by a vertical line, bisected by a number of diagonal lines, and topped by a horizontal line. The number of diagonal lines indicates the number of yarn wraps before the hook is inserted into the fabric.

Stitch height chart

This is a list of stitches and the number of wraps around the hook each requires; before the hook is inserted into the fabric.

Stitch	No. of wraps
Slip stitch (sl st)	0
Single crochet (sc)	0
Half double crochet (hdc)	1
Double crochet (dc)	1
Treble crochet (tr)	2
Double treble (dtr)	3
Triple treble (trtr)	4
Quadruple treble (qutr)	5

Working a crochet stitch taller than a treble crochet stitch

To work a taller crochet stitch, wrap the yarn over the hook the number of times indicated. Insert the hook into the work. Wrap the yarn over the hook and draw through. Wrap the yarn over the hook and draw through two loops. Repeat the process of wrapping the yarn around the hook and drawing it through two loops until only one loop remains on the hook.

Tip   For single crochet, double crochet, and treble crochet, the stitch name gives an indication of the number of times the yarn needs to be wrapped around the hook and drawn through two loops before the stitch is completed. For instance, for a treble crochet it is three times.

Stitch placement

One of the joys of crochet is the variety of different ways a crochet stitch can be placed on a fabric. It's usual to work crochet stitches under both loops of the stitches made on the previous row but stitches can also be worked through either the front or back top loops of the stitches, between stitches, around stitches, through chain spaces as well as through back bars and stitch stems. Each will take the fabric in a different direction.

Working into a chain space

Stitches can be worked into a chain space in two different ways. They can be worked into the chain loops or into the space under the chain loops. The first will restrict the movement of the stitch, the second will allow the stitch some freedom of movement depending on the number of stitches worked into the space and the width of the chain space. A group of stitches or cluster worked into a chain space will be flatter with a broader base because the stitches will spread out along the chain. A cluster worked into a stitch will have a narrower base and so will fan out. If a large number of stitches is worked into a single point a raised textured may be created.

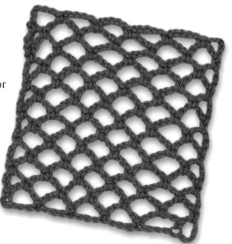

▲ Mesh fabrics

The movement of stitches worked into a chain is contained only by the stitches immediately to the left, right, and on following rows. The chain stitch structure is particularly vulnerable to stretch and variations in gauge. If the fabric you are creating does not lie flat or pulls against itself then adjust the chain lengths.

Working into stitches

Unless otherwise instructed, it is usual to work crochet stitches under both loops of the stitches made on the previous row. However, by working under one loop, either the back or the front, the remaining loop becomes a horizontal bar and the drape of the fabric is improved.

Crochet stitches can also be worked into a part of the stitch called the back bar. This is a horizontal strand of yarn below the top loops of a stitch. It is most pronounced on half double crochet stitches (see page 23) but can also be found on taller stitches. If worked on taller stitches, a looser gauge can be helpful.

Occasionally, a pattern will suggest that a stitch is worked through the stem of a stitch. Insert the hook from front to back through the looser twisted strands in the middle of a stitch and complete the desired stitch. Depending on the height and position of the stitch in the stem a flap of fabric is created on the side facing away as the stitch is worked.

Working into the front or back loop of a stitch

Working into the front loop Working into the front of the stitch creates slight horizontal ridges on the side facing away as the stitch is worked. To work into the front of a row of stitches, insert the hook under only the front loops of the stitches on the previous row.

Working into the back loop Working into the back of the stitch creates a strongly ridged fabric on the side facing as the stitch is worked. To work into the back loop of a row of stitches, insert the hook under only the back loop of the stitches on the previous row.

Working spike stitches

Spiked or dropped stitches are worked individually into the space between stitches but also over other stitches. Usually over a background fabric made up of single crochet stitches. As well as adding texture to a fabric, if the spike stitches are worked in a contrasting color to the background fabric interesting color combinations can be achieved. Spike stitches reduce the drape of a fabric and create a denser fabric.

1 Insert the hook, as directed, through the fabric to the wrong side.

2 Wrap the yarn around the hook, and draw the loop through to the front. Lengthen the loop to the height of the working row. Take care not to pull the loop too tightly as this will distort the fabric. Drawing too much yarn through may make the yarn strands prone to snagging.

3 Wrap the yarn around the hook, and draw it through both loops on the hook.

Tip Working a striped fabric of any stitch in the spaces between the stitches on the previous row creates a strip of fabric with both colors, and the drape is lighter than that of a fabric where the stitches are worked into the stitches of the row below.

Post or relief stitches

Post stitches are created by working a stitch such as a double crochet stitch or treble stitch around the post (stem or body) of a stitch made on a previous row. This creates a heavily textured surface.

Working post or relief double crochet stitches

Front post or relief stitch Wrap the yarn around the hook, insert the hook from front to back, from right to left around the back of the stitch. Wrap the yarn over the hook and draw it and the hook back around the post of the stitch and complete the double crochet stitch.

Back post or relief stitch Wrap the yarn around the hook, insert the hook from back to front of the work, from right to left around the back of the stitch. Wrap the yarn over the hook and draw it and the hook back around the post of the stitch and complete the double crochet stitch.

Crossed stitches

Crossed stitches are when stitches along a row are not worked in sequence but stitches are skipped and then worked later around the front or back of the stitches just worked. For wider crossed stitch groups, a progression of stitches of varying heights may be used.

Working in rows

Working back and forth in rows can produce a flat fabric for which there are numerous stitch patterns or combinations described. Although the difference between the front and back of most stitches is subtle, the crochet fabric has texture when the stitches are simply worked back and forth. Even using just one stitch and perhaps some creative stitch placements, there are endless beautiful fabric possibilities.

Turning chain guide

The list below shows the correct number of chain stitches needed to make a turn for each stitch. If you have a tendency to work chain stitches very tightly, you may need to work an extra chain in order to keep the edges of your work from becoming too tight.

Stitch	No. of ch sts to turn
Slip stitch (sl st)	0
Single crochet (sc)	1
Half double crochet (hdc)	2
Double crochet (dc)	3
Treble crochet (tr)	4
Double treble (dtr)	5
Triple treble (trtr)	6
Quadruple treble (qutr)	7

Creating a flat fabric

For a flat fabric, some means of getting the hook up to the correct height for the intended next stitch is required. For working in rows with a side edge at right angles to the direction of work, a turning chain is used. They are the chain stitches at the beginning of each row.

Usually, the turning chain is counted as the first stitch of the row, except when working single crochet where the single turning chain is ignored. For example, ch 3 (counts as 1 dc) at the beginning of a row or round means that the turning or starting chain contains three chain stitches and these are counted as the equivalent of one double crochet stitch. A turning chain may be longer than the number required for the stitch, and in which case it counts as one stitch plus a number of chains.

Usually a pattern will indicate what the turning chain represents in bracketed copy.

At the end of the row, the final stitch is usually worked into the turning chain worked on the previous row. The final stitch may be worked into the top chain of the chain (the last chain worked before the first stitch) or into another specified stitch of the chain.

Stripes

Simple horizontal stripes worked in two, three, or more colors add zing to plain crochet—the stripes can be strongly contrasting in color or the effect can be more subtle by using a restricted palette of shades of one color plus one or more coordinating colors. Single crochet, half double crochet, and double crochet stitches all look good worked in stripes.

▲ Ripple stitches
or chevron stripes

Chevron stripes are worked in a similar way to plain horizontal stripes, but stitches are added and subtracted at regular intervals along each row. This forms a pattern of regular peaks and troughs separated by blocks of stitches— a zigzag.

Joining in a new length of yarn or changing colors

This can be either joining in a new length of the same yarn or the joining in of a second yarn or color to create a stripe. Join the yarn at the end of the row. Leave the last stage of the final stitch incomplete, loop the new yarn round the hook and pull it through the stitches on the hook to complete the stitch, then turn and work the next row with the new yarn. Cut the yarn no longer in use, leaving an end of about 4 in. (10 cm).

Working in rounds

Working crochet in flat rounds rather than backward and forward in straight rows offers a new range of possibilities to make colorful and intricate pieces of crochet called motifs or medallions. Crochet motifs are worked outward from a central ring. Evenly spaced increases result in a flat, circular motif, but when the increases are grouped together to make corners, the resulting motif can be a square, hexagon, or other flat shape.

Creating a flat fabric

For a flat fabric, the hook has to be the correct height or in the correct position for the intended next stitch. For working in round either a starting chain or turning chain can be used (see page 32). A starting chain is where the work is not turned but continues in the same direction as the last round. A turning chain is where the work is turned after the round is completed. Each produces a different fabric. If the motif has an undulating or lacy edge, a series of slip stitches can also be used to get the hook into the correct position. Usually one of these two methods is used at the beginning of every round.

To create a flat fabric the number of stitches has to increase on each round (pages 66–67).

Making a ring of stitches

Begin making the foundation ring by working a short length of foundation chain (page 18), with a slightly looser slip knot than usual, as specified in the pattern. Join the chains into a ring by working a slip stitch into the first stitch of the foundation chain. Gently tighten the first stitch by pulling the loose yarn end with your left hand.

Making a yarn ring

1 This method of making a foundation ring is useful because the yarn end is enclosed with the first round of stitches and will not need to be woven in later. Begin by holding the yarn end between the thumb and first finger of your left hand and wind the yarn several times round the tip of your finger.

2 Carefully slip the yarn ring off your finger. Inserting the hook into the ring, pull a loop of yarn through and work a single crochet stitch to secure the ring.

Working into a yarn ring

1 Work the number of turning chains specified in the pattern. Inserting the hook into the space at the center of the ring each time, work the number of stitches into the ring as specified in the pattern.

2 Join the first and last stitches of the round together by working a slip stitch into the top of the turning chain.

Shaping

Shaping by adding or subtracting one or two stitches can take place at intervals along a row of crochet—this is known as working internal increases or decreases. When stitches are added or subtracted at the beginning and end of specified rows, this is known as working external increases or decreases. They are not always written out, in pattern copy, in a way that they can be easily recognized as such but as clusters or decorative stitches.

Increasing

The simplest method of adding stitches at the beginning or end of the row or at intervals along a row, is to work two or more stitches into a space previously occupied by one stitch on the previous row.

Making a neat edge when shaping

At the start of a row, work the first stitch and then work the increase.

At the end of the row, work until two stitches remain (the last stitch will probably be the turning chain from the previous row). Work the increase into the penultimate stitch, then work the last stitch as usual.

Working an external increase at the start of a row

1 To increase several stitches at one time, you will need to add extra foundation chains at the appropriate end of the row. To add stitches at the beginning of a row, work the required number of extra chains at the end of the previous row. Don't forget to add the correct number of turning chains (page 32) for the stitch you are using.

2 Turn and work back along the extra chains, then continue to work the row in the usual way.

Working an external increase at the end of a row

1 Leave the last few stitches of the row unworked. Remove the hook. Join a length of yarn to the last stitch of the row and work the required number of extra chains, then fasten off the yarn.

2 Insert the hook back into the row and continue, working extra stitches across the chains. Turn and work the next row in the usual way.

Decreasing

Skipping stitches is a very effective way of reducing the number of stitches along a row. This can take the obvious form of skipping a stitch or not working it, or it can mean some judicious chain stitches distributing one pattern repeat over the space of two pattern repeats. If working decreases on a complex stitch pattern, wherever possible allow the natural line of the stitch pattern to dictate the decreases. A few extra stitches may be required to fill in some holes but they need not be worked on the following rows. For clothing a stitch pattern with a short repeat is best for a well-fitted garment.

Working an internal decrease by skipping a stitch

The simplest method of removing a single stitch at intervals along a row of crochet is by skipping one stitch of the previous row.

Working an internal decrease in single crochet

Decrease one stitch by working two stitches together (sc2tog). Leave the first stitch incomplete (two loops on the hook), draw the yarn through the next stitch (three loops on the hook). Yarn over and pull through all three loops to finish. Decrease two stitches by working three stitches together (sc3tog).

Working an internal decrease in double crochet

Decrease one double crochet stitch by working two stitches together (known as dc2tog). Work the number of stitches, indicated until the stage before the final yarnover completes the stitch. Additional instructions will be given in the pattern as to where to place the stitches. Yarn over and pull through all the loops to finish the decrease. This decrease technique can be applied using other stitches such as single crochet stitches (sctog) and trebles (trtog).

To make a neat ease one stitch in from the edge in the same way as a single or double increase (pages 36–37).

Two stitches can be decreased in the same way by working three double crochet stitches together (dc3tog).

Working an external decrease at the start of a row

To decrease several stitches at one time at the beginning of a row, turn, work a slip stitch into each of the stitches to be decreased, then work the appropriate turning chain and continue along the row.

Working an external decrease at the end of a row

At the end of the row, simply leave the stitches to be decreased unworked, work the appropriate turning chain, turn, and continue along the row.

Fastening off

Fastening off is very different from finishing which involves the final stretching and steaming, or blocking, of a piece of crochet. The question is when to weave in the yarn ends. Some people prefer to weave in yarn ends before blocking a piece of crochet because the blocking process helps to "bed" them—or embed them. However, be careful not to restrict the stretch of the crochet fabric with tightly woven in yarn ends.

Fastening off yarn

Weaving in yarn ends

To fasten off the yarn at the end of a piece of crochet, cut the yarn 6 in. (15 cm) from the last stitch, and pull the yarn end through the stitch with the hook. For slippery yarn, work one chain stitch with the yarn end before pulling the yarn through the chain stitch. Gently pull the yarn end to tighten the chain stitch and weave the end in on the wrong side of the work.

Undo the knot securing the two colors, thread the needle with one color, and weave the end into the wrong side of the same color of stripe.

Weaving a yarn end along the top edge of a row of stitches

To weave a yarn end in at the top of the work, thread the end in a large tapestry needle. Weave the end through several stitches on the wrong side of the work. Trim the remaining yarn.

Weaving a yarn end along the lower edge of a row of stitches

To weave a yarn end in along the lower edge, thread the end in a tapestry needle and draw it through several stitches on the wrong side of the work. Trim the remaining yarn.

Finishing off the final rounds of a motif

1 Cut the yarn, leaving an end of about 4 in. (10 cm) and draw it though the last stitch. With right side facing, thread the end in a large tapestry needle and take it under both loops of the stitch next to the turning chain.

2 Pull the needle through, insert it into the center of the last stitch of the round. On the wrong side, pull the needle through to complete the stitch, adjust the length of the stitch to close the round, then weave in the end on the wrong side in the usual way.

Gauge

The term "gauge" refers to the number of stitches and rows contained in a given width and length of crochet fabric. Crochet patterns include a recommended gauge and it's important that you match this gauge exactly so your work comes out the right size. Gauge can be affected by the size and brand of the crochet hook, the type of yarn used, the type of stitch pattern, and the gauge of an individual worker.

Hook variations

Hooks can vary widely in shape and size even though they may all be branded with the same number or letter. You'll probably find that you prefer the feel of one type of hook, so it's a good idea to buy several consecutive sizes once you've made your choice. Always use the same hook for working both the gauge sample and the finished item.

Yarn variations

Two yarns with the same description (e.g. sport or worsted) and fiber content made by different manufacturers will vary slightly in thickness. The color of yarn you choose may also affect gauge as a result of the different dyes used in manufacture.

If you cannot obtain the exact yarn used in the pattern, you will probably be able to find one that is similar. Read the pattern instructions and make a note of the gauge, hook size, fiber content, and yardage, if quoted. Try to find a substitute yarn that matches all these criteria as closely as possible, paying particular attention to the gauge. Buy one ball of the yarn and experiment with making gauge samples until your sample matches the gauge in the pattern (see right).

Making a gauge sample

Read the pattern instructions to find the recommended gauge. Work a generously sized sample 6–8 in. (15–20 cm) wide. If you are working a stitch pattern, choose a number of foundation chains to suit the stitch repeat. Work in the required pattern until the piece is 6–8 in. (15–20 cm) long. Fasten off the yarn. Block the gauge sample using the method suited to the yarn composition (pages 98–99) and allow to dry.

Measuring a gauge sample

Lay the sample right side up on a flat surface and use a solid ruler and pins to measure 4 in. (10 cm) horizontally across a row of stitches and vertically up a line of stitches. Make a note of the number of stitches and rows (including partial stitches and rows) between the pins. This is the gauge to 4 in. (10 cm).

Gauge information may be quoted as a multiple of the pattern repeat, rather than as a set number of rows and stitches, in which case, count the number of repeats for the given distance.

How to adjust the gauge

If you have more stitches or pattern repeats in your gauge sample, your gauge is too tight and you should make another sample using a larger hook size.

If you have less stitches or pattern repeats in your gauge sample, your gauge is too loose and you should make another sample using a smaller hook size.

Block the new sample as before and repeat this process until your gauge matches that given in the pattern.

Tip Remember to check the yardage of the original yarn and any substituted yarn. As a general rule, man-made yarns are lighter and have a longer yardage than woolen yarns. Cotton and cotton-blend yarns are usually heavy and will have a shorter yardage than man-made or woolen yarns. When in doubt, it's a good idea to buy an extra ball of yarn.

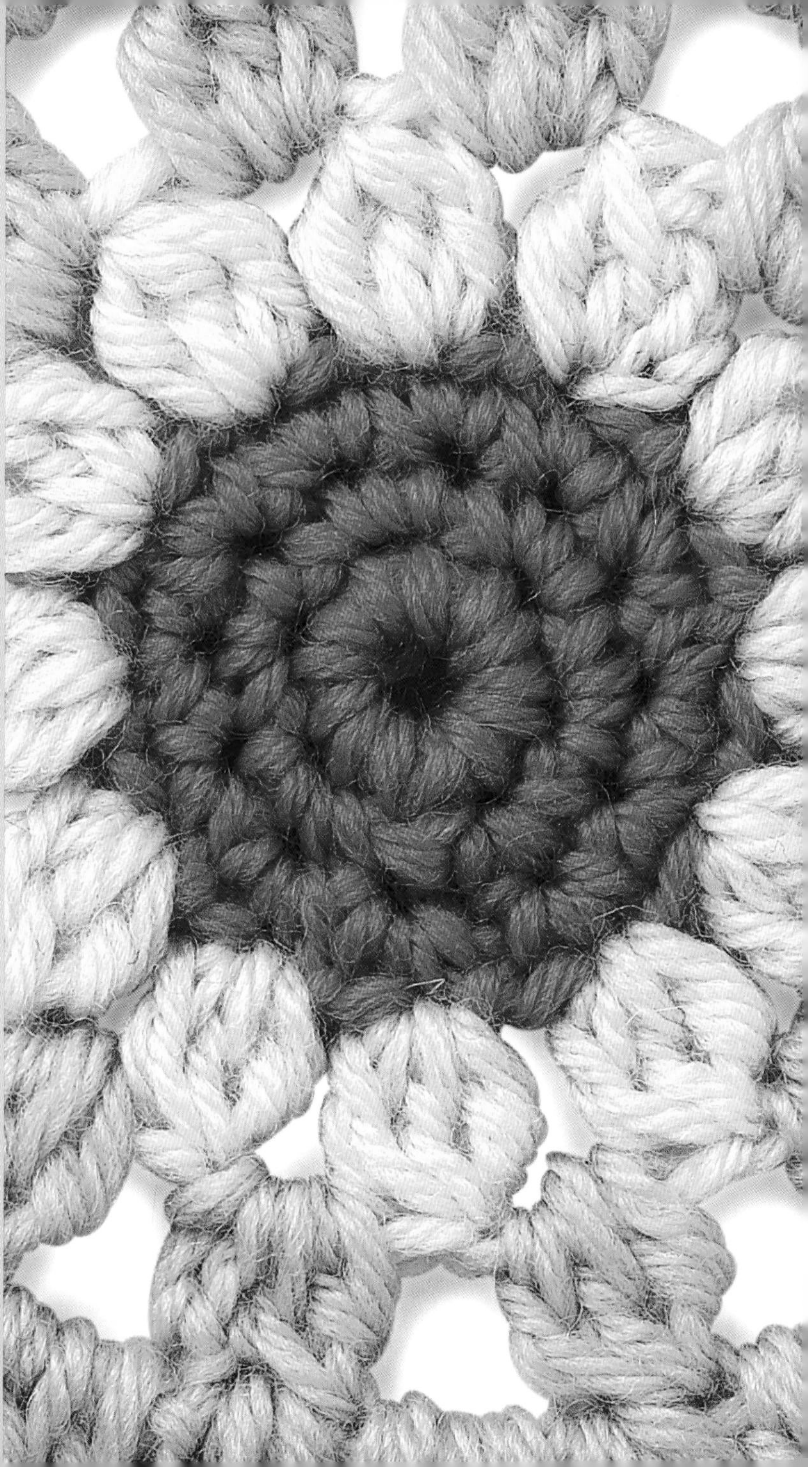

Beyond Basic Crochet

Clusters

Any combination of stitches can be joined into a cluster by leaving the last loop of each stitch on the hook as it is made, then securing the loops together at the end. This technique is used as a method of decreasing one or more stitches (page 38) but it also makes attractive textured stitches in its own right. Puff stitches, bobbles, and popcorns are all cluster variations, but they are worked using different methods.

Basic cluster

Joining two, three, or more stitches at the top as you work forms a group called a cluster. The stitches can be of the same type or different. Use this technique for decorative purposes or to decrease stitches.

Working a basic cluster

1 To work a three double crochet cluster, yarn over hook, work the first stitch, omitting the last stage to leave two loops on the hook. Work the second stitch in the same way. You now have three loops on the hook.

2 Work the last stitch of the cluster in the same way, resulting in four loops on the hook. Wind the yarn over the hook. Draw the yarn through the four loops on the hook to complete the cluster and secure the loops.

Basic bobble

A bobble is a cluster of between three and five stitches worked into the same stitch and closed at the top. Bobbles are usually worked on wrong side rows and surrounded by shorter stitches to throw them into relief.

Working a basic bobble

1 To make a five stitch bobble, wrap the yarn over the hook, work the first stitch, omitting the last stage to leave two loops on the hook. Work the second and third stitches in the same way. You now have four loops on the hook.

2 Work the remaining two stitches of the bobble in the same way, resulting in six loops on the hook. Wind the yarn over the hook and draw it through the six loops to secure them. Gently poke the bobble through to the other side of the work as you draw the securing loop through.

3 (Right side) On the following row, work a row of single crochet, taking care to work one stitch into the securing stitch at the top of each bobble.

Basic popcorn

A popcorn stitch is a cluster of stitches (the number may vary), which may be worked into one place or over a short distance and is folded and closed at the top. If the popcorn begins to loosen then secure with an extra chain before continuing to work the crochet fabric.

Working a basic popcorn

1 To make a popcorn with four separate double crochet stitches, work a group of four double crochet stitches.

2 Take the hook out of the working loop and insert it under both loops of the first double crochet stitch in the group.

3 Pick up the working loop with the hook and draw it through to fold the group of stitches and close it at the top. The popcorn is now complete.

Tip A popcorn may be made from a group of separate stitches as above, or the group can share one stitch at the base. Like a bobble this gives a more raised effect. Popcorns worked into chain spaces are usually worked by the first method.

Basic puff stitch

A puff stitch is a cluster of half double crochet stitches worked in the same place—the number of stitches in each puff can vary. A cluster of half double crochet stitches can also be worked over a short distance but some extra care may be required to keep the loops neat and smooth.

Working a basic puff stitch

1 Wrap the yarn over the hook, insert the hook into the stitch, yarn over hook again and draw a loop through.

2 Repeat this step as specified, inserting the hook into the same stitch.

3 Wrap the yarn over the hook and draw it through all seven loops on the hook. Work an extra chain stitch at the top of the puff to complete the stitch.

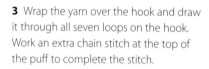

Tip A stitch pattern made up of predominately either half double crochet clusters or puff stitches is often reversible. Puff stitches are also light and soft which makes them an excellent choice for blankets and afghans.

Shells and fans

Shell stitches are formed from three or more stitches that have been placed into the same stitch but unlike a cluster they are not secured at the top. This creates a triangular group of stitches that look like a tiny clam. A fan is nearly any other curved group of stitches. A fan can be worked over several rows with its base on the first row a shell or it can be stitches worked into a group of stitches or a chain space where the stitches fan out.

It is important to note that on following rows each stitch of a shell or a fan still counts as one stitch. The stitches can, however, be referred to as a group. Occasionally in patterns an instruction may be given to work into the center stitch of a shell or fan or to skip a shell or fan. Usually chains or stitches at either side of a shell are missed to compensate for the space taken up by the shell or fan and allow them to spread out. So shells and fans are not necessarily an indication of a decorative increase.

Working a basic shell
Skip the stated number of chains or stitches and work the first stitch of the shell, in this case a double crochet, into the indicated chain or stitch. Work the remaining stitches of the shell into the same place as the previous stitch and again skip the stated number of chains or stitches.

Working a fan stitch over several rows

1 On the first pattern row work a shell as indicated. On the next row, increase as directed into the top of the stitches forming the shell. This creates a wider band of stitches. On the next pattern row the instructions may indicate that the fan has been completed by instructing a short chain worked into the center stitch or skipping the fan stitches.

2 Alternatively the fan may continue on following rows with further increases worked on each row.

Working a fan stitch into a chain space

Many lacy patterns combine shells, fans, and chain spaces. To work into a chain space, insert the hook into a chain space and not the stitch forming the chain strand. This allows the stitches free movement.

Loopy stitches

Loopy stitches fall into two categories: the first is where short lengths of crochet chain are formed into loops (astrakhan stitch); the second is where extended loops are made from the working yarn (loop stitch). A variation on the second can be used to create beaded loops. Both types of stitch make a delightful texture and are good for making accessories such as scarves and hats, or for working collars and cuffs to trim a plain garment.

Astrakhan stitch

Unlike most other crochet stitches, astrakhan stitch is worked back and forth without turning the work. With the right side facing and working right to left a plain row of stitches is worked. The stitches are usually double crochet stitches but for a denser fabric single crochet

stitches can be used and for a fabric with more drape and more widely spaced rows of loops, treble crochet can be used. This plain row is followed by a row of loops. The loop row is worked from left to right and is made up of short chain lengths that are then secured with slip stitches into the front loops of the stitches from the previous plain row. The frequency of the loops can be varied from one for each stitch to one loop for three or four stitches. Choose a chain length that works well with the yarn and the loop spacing along the row. Work the next plain row into the back loops of the last plain row. Just repeat the last two rows. This fabric is thick and incredibly tactile although it can be quite heavy and so it is important to balance the three components of yarn, loop length, and plain row stitch carefully.

Loop stitch

Loop stitches are worked on wrong-side rows of single crochet by extending a loop of yarn with your finger and securing it. Loop stitches can be worked in every stitch along the row, in groups, or alternately with plain single crochet stitches.

Loop stitches do vary slightly in how they are worked so it is important to check the pattern instructions carefully before working the stitch. Basically, with the wrong side of the work facing, the hook is inserted into the next stitch as usual. A finger is used to pull out the working yarn to make a loop of the desired size, and then both strands of the loop are picked up with the hook and drawn through the crochet fabric. The loop is then secured by wrapping the working yarn over the hook and drawing the yarn through all three loops on the hook.

Making beaded loops

1 The beaded loops hang down between two stitches on the side facing away as you work. Thread the beads onto the yarn. Then, working on a wrong side row, work to the position of the beaded loop, slide a number of beads along the yarn until they lie snugly at the base of the hook.

2 Insert the hook into the next stitch and work the next stitch. The more beads the longer and heavier the loop.

Applying beads

Beads can be applied to crochet at the same time as the stitches are being worked. They can be threaded onto the yarn and positioned between the stitches or half way through a taller bead. The threading procedure can also be avoided and the beads individually hooked onto a crochet fabric as it is worked. For heavily beaded evening purses, the single crochet stitch is the most popular because it best supports the weight of the beads.

First of all a word about the beads. Take a length of yarn with you when choosing beads, match the size of the holes in the beads to the thickness of your yarn; small beads are best on fine yarns, and larger beads on chunky yarns. If you can, thread a few beads onto the yarn and check the color. This is especially helpful with glass beads. Finally, think carefully about the weight of the beads and their durability in a project.

Tip Alternatively, to thread beads onto a length of yarn, bend a piece of fine wire in half, place the last few inches of yarn in the fold and use the wire to hold it in place. Push the two ends of the wire together through a bead and slide the bead down the wire and along the yarn.

Threading beads onto yarn with a needle

If the beads are to be threaded onto the yarn and they are to be arranged in a particular color or size pattern, the beads need to be threaded on in reverse order—the last bead to be crocheted on the yarn first. Thread the beads onto a loop of strong thread—buttonhole thread is ideal. Slot the end of the yarn through the thread loop and slide the beads from the thread onto the yarn.

Working a beaded foundation chain

Thread the beads onto the yarn. Make a slip knot, slide the bead along the yarn to the base of the hook and wrap the yarn around the hook. Draw the yarn through the loop. The bead is at the back of the chain as part of the back bump.

Adding beads individually to a crochet fabric

Adding beads individually on the right-side rows with a second, smaller hook is useful for "spot" beading where small groups or individual beads are scattered here and there on the crochet fabric.

Threading beads with a hook

1 Work the next stitch until there are two loops on the hook. Remove the hook from the loop nearest the tip of the hook. Place a bead onto a smaller hook, slip it through the loose loop and draw the loop through the bead with the hook.

2 Return the beaded yarn loop onto the main hook and complete the stitch.

Beading with single crochet

1 Slide the bead down the yarn until it rests snugly against the right side of your work at the base of the hook.

2 Keeping the bead in position, insert hook in next stitch and draw yarn through so there are two loops on the hook. Wrap the yarn over the hook again and draw it through to complete the stitch.

▲ **Alternate beads**
Beads of one color are arranged alternately to make this elegant beaded pattern. Use matte beads, like the ones shown, or choose from metallic and glitter types to add more sparkle.

▲ **Sequin stripes**
Sequins can be added in the same way as beads. Ensure that the sequins have been threaded onto the yarn so that the convex of the sequin faces the ball of yarn and is flat against the crochet fabric before it is secured.

Beaded increases and decreases

Adding beads to an increase or decrease makes a feature of the shaping and the weight of beads will improve the drape of the fabric along the same line as the beads. Use the beads as a reminder as to when to add an increase or decrease to crochet fabric. Thread the beads onto the yarn before making the slip knot and working the foundation chain.

Working a beaded double increase

Work the first stitch of increase, slide one bead along the yarn to the base of the hook, work the second stitch of the increase into the same place.

Working a beaded double decrease

1 Insert the hook into the first decrease stitch position, wrap the yarn over the hook and draw the loop through.

2 Slide one bead along the yarn to the base of the hook, insert the hook into the second stitch position, and complete the decrease.

Crochet Fabrics

59

Understanding patterns

Crochet pattern instructions are laid out in a logical sequence, although the terminology can look rather complicated. The most important thing to remember when following a pattern is to check that you start off with the correct number of stitches in the foundation row or ring, and then work through the instructions row-by-row exactly as stated. To save space, abbreviations are used for stitches and frequently used phrases.

Standard abbreviations

ch(s)	chain(s)
sl st	slip stitch
sc	single crochet
hdc	half double crochet
dc	double crochet
tr	treble or triple crochet
st(s)	stitch(es)
sp(s)	space(s)
lp(s)	loop(s)
rep	repeat
sk	skip
yo	yarn over hook
rem	remaining
cont	continue
alt	alternate
beg	beginning
foll	following
patt	pattern

See also page 180.

In addition to the standard abbreviations given left, there may be special abbreviations for the particular pattern you are working. These will be explained with the relevant pattern. Symbols are also used such as: brackets; asterisks; daggers; and stars. These help avoid the repetition of instructions. The instructions will be phrased slightly differently depending on whether square brackets or symbols are used.

Tip Each stitch pattern worked in rows is written using a specific number of pattern rows and the sequence is repeated until the crochet is the correct length. When working a complicated stitch pattern, always make a note of exactly which row you are working.

Brackets

The sequence of stitches enclosed inside brackets [] must be worked as instructed. For example, [1 dc into the next 3 sts, ch 2] 4 times means that you will work the three double crochet stitches and the two chains four times in all.

Parentheses

Parentheses () contain extra information, not instructions to be worked—such as stitches for different sizes. You may also find a number enclosed in parentheses at the end of a row or round—this indicates the total number of stitches to be worked in that particular row or round.

Asterisks, daggers, and stars

Asterisks are the most widely used symbol in crochet instructions, but the other two may appear in complex patterns. Any of the symbols may be used to indicate that you must repeat the sequence of stitches (or the instructions) that follow the symbol. These symbols can fulfill a similar function to square brackets but although some publications use them in preference to brackets they do tend to indicate a longer repeat.

Charted patterns

With the exception of filet crochet patterns, which are always worked from a chart (page 82), most crochet patterns found across the English-speaking world use written instructions to describe the method of working. The majority of crochet patterns originating from Europe (with the exception of Britain) are charts using symbols to indicate the different stitches and how they are placed. The symbols have been standardized so the same ones can be used throughout the world. A charted pattern still contains some written instructions, but the stitch patterns are shown in a visual form. Charted instructions also solve the problem of translating lengthy written instructions from one language to another.

To use a charted pattern, first familiarize yourself with the different symbols and their meanings (see page 180). These are explained in a key at the side of the chart. Each symbol represents a single instruction or stitch, and indicates exactly where to work the stitch. Follow the numerical sequence on the chart whether you are working in rows or rounds. In the same way as when using a written pattern, keep a note of which row or round you are working on.

Motifs

The motifs are mostly worked outward from a central ring (see pages 34–35) and can be circular, square, triangular, hexagonal, or octagonal in shape, and solid or lacy in appearance. They are worked and joined using the same techniques as other crochet fabrics to make afghans, shawls, and wraps, as well as simply shaped garments. In addition there are a few techniques which help lacy motifs in particular keep their singular charm.

Lace motifs

Lace motifs are light, pretty, and delicate to look at when worked in lightweight yarns, and are perfect for making shawls, wraps, and stoles. Lace motifs are usually joined together on the final pattern round as you work, eliminating the need for sewing and creating a join more in keeping with the rest of the motif. The joins are usually worked through a picot or loop which can be added to any block. With a block only joined at a few points the drape of a fabric of even dense blocks is improved. It's usual to join several motifs to make a strip, then add further motifs along one long edge of the strip until you have two strips joined together. Keep adding motifs until you have joined the required number of strips together.

▲ **Spanish lace**
This motif looks very different when joined to its neighbor. Work several of the same motif before making a final choice. See page 159 for the pattern for this motif.

Changing the hook position with slip stitches

Working in slip stitch (page 19) across one or more stitches is a useful way of changing the position of yarn and hook on a round. Pattern directions may refer to this technique as "slip stitch across" or "slip stitch into." Here, slip stitches are being worked into the edge of a petal in order to move the hook and yarn from the valley between two petals to the tip of one petal, ready to work the next sequence of stitches.

Making and working into a chain loop

1 Long chain loops (they may also be described as chain spaces or chain arches) are an integral part of lace motif patterns. They are sometimes used as a foundation for stitches worked in the following round, or they may form a visible part of the design. Work chain loops as evenly as possible, anchoring them by working a slip stitch or single crochet into the previous round.

2 When a chain loop is worked as a foundation on one row, stitches are worked over the chains on the following row. Insert the hook into the space below the chain loop to work each stitch, not directly into individual chain stitches.

Joining lace motifs

1 Complete the first motif. Work the second motif up to the last round, then work the first side of the last round, ending at the specified point where the first join will be made, in this case it is halfway along a chain loop at the corner of the motif.

2 Place the first and second motifs together, with wrong sides facing, ready to work the next side of the second motif. Join the chain loops with a single crochet stitch, then complete the loop on the second motif. Continue along the same side of the second motif, joining chain loops together each time with single crochet stitches.

3 After all the loops along one side are joined, complete the second motif in the usual way. Work further motifs in the same way, joining the required number together to make a strip of motifs.

4 Work the first motif of the second strip, stopping when you have reached the joining point. Place against the side of the top motif in the first strip (wrong sides facing) and join the chain loops as before. When you reach the point where three corner loops meet, work the single crochet into the stitch joining the two existing motifs.

5 Work the second motif of the second strip, stopping when you have reached the joining point. Place against the side of the first motif in the second strip (wrong sides facing) and join the chain loops as before. When you reach the point where all four corner loops meet, work the single crochet into the stitch joining the first two motifs.

6 Now join the next side of the motif to the adjacent side of the first strip, working single crochet stitches into chain loops as before. Complete the remaining sides of the motif. Continue working in the same way until you have made and joined the required number of motifs.

Circle motifs

Mistakes happen and things go wrong but the trick is to identify the mistake and put it right. A circle is the base of many motif shapes and understanding of its construction will help solve many problems. Of course these are all rough guidelines and increases can become part of clusters and corners be made from more than chain loops, however, a number of the basic principles often remain the same.

Working a crochet circle

The easiest way to create a circle design in crochet is to work from the center and increase every round until the desired size is reached. The number of increases a motif may require in each round can vary from ten stitches, which may create a circle that pulls in to the center, to about sixteen stitches.

▲ Circle motif
Stripes and texture can be added to the shape as long as the number of stitches increases with each round.

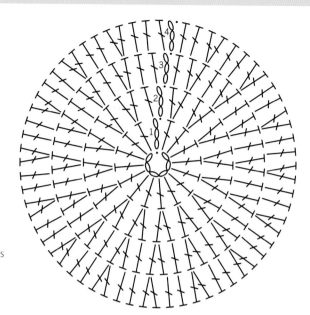

Double crochet circle chart ▶

The numbers of stitches in each round increase by sixteen stitches.

The circle can either start with a foundation ring (see page 34) or a yarn ring (see page 35). The first round usually has about half the number of stitches as there will be increases in each round although five stitches would be unusual. The second round usually doubles the number of increases in the first round, again except in the case of a first round of five stitches where there may also be some chain loops. Then to create a flat circle, increases are worked on every round into the first stitch of the increase on the previous round. If the edge of the circle curls up, there are not enough increases, and if a frill appears there are too may increases for the stitch pattern and gauge used.

Other shapes

Other shapes can be worked from the center in the same way. As for a circle they start with a foundation ring or yarn loop. The first round usually has a number of stitches which is a multiple of the number of sides the shape will have. Increases follow a similar pattern to that of a circle. On the second round or third round, chain loops are usually added for the corners. On the following rounds, the corner position will be maintained with more stitches and chain loops or groups of stitches. The other increases needed to keep the shape flat are worked in between the corners with the extra stitches becoming part of the corner or side design as the motif extends outward.

Square motifs

Square motifs are very popular in afghan and blanket construction. As long as enough squares of any one size are made, they tessellate easily to create a range of shapes. There are a variety of ways that a square motif shape can be created and once the shaping pattern is established they are a wonderful way to experiment with new techniques and stitch patterns, or simply doodle with yarn and a hook.

▲ Radiating stripes

As long as the corner increases are maintained, the stitches in between can follow any stitch pattern. To preserve the square shape any increase of stitches along the edges must be temporary.

Working from the center out

A square block worked from the center starts in the same way as a circle (see page 66–67). The number of stitches worked into the foundation ring, including the turning chain, is often twelve or sixteen. On the following round, the corners will either be created by working three or five stitches or by working a stitch, a chain, and another stitch into four evenly spaced stitches in the round. On the following rounds, the increases keep the fabric flat and the corners are maintained by creating twelve or sixteen extra stitches on each round evenly over the four corners. This can be done by working stitches into the center stitch of the corner stitches or the corner chain loop of

◀ Diagonal stripes
If a square block is worked from corner to corner and stripes of color are introduced the stripes will run diagonally across the square.

Working from corner to corner

Squares worked from corner to corner usually start with two stitches into a slip knot. Then on the following rows increases are made at either end or one end of every row until the selvage edge equals that of the size of block required. Decreases are worked at either end or one end of every row until no stitches remain. On the single crochet swatch shown above, the increases and decreases are worked one stitch in from the edge at both the beginning and end of the row. Working a square block from corner to corner has several advantages. First is that mixing and matching different yarn weights in one project does not require lots of gauge swatches. If a block is worked with a heavier weight yarn it will simply require fewer increase rows before the number of stitches is decreased. Secondly, half squares are easy to make. Once the selvage of a block reaches the right length the yarn is fastened off.

each corner of the previous round. The corner chain loop counts as one stitch.

To create a half-square block, work in rows and only half of the stitches prescribed for each round. At the end of each row, turn and work back across the stitches just worked. A half block can divide from corner to corner or from the middle of an edge to the middle of an edge. This is defined by the position of the corners on the second row. For a block divided from corner to corner, each row has to start and finish with a corner. The edge corners should be half the number of stitches of a full corner plus or minus half a stitch. A test swatch may be required to get the shaping absolutely correct.

◀ **Double crochet mitered block**
Single crochet stitches and half double crochet stitches work equally well.

Working from the corner out

This type of block usually starts with a group of stitches worked into a foundation ring or slip knot. A square block worked from the corner out has many of the benefits of a block worked from corner to corner. Once the shaping patterns is established the pattern is simply repeated until the selvage matches that of the side of the block required. It too is worked in rows back and forth but the difference is that the increases are arranged in the center of the row. The same number of extra stitches are required on each row but they are worked into a center corner stitch or corner chain loop which also has to be worked on each row. So if a block worked from point to point needs two stitches on each row, a mitered block worked from the corner needs two new stitches and a new group of stitches to create the corner.

A half block can be created by positioning half the increase stitches and half a corner on one edge.

Tip For a neater edge for easier seaming, work a round of stitches around the entire block, working corner stitch groups into the corner stitches.

Working from the outside edges in

A square worked from the outside edges in starts with a foundation chain of the required length for two sides of the block. For this kind of block a gauge swatch is required. It is worked in rows back and forth but the difference is that there decreases arranged in the center of the row. For single crochet the number of decreases is usually two stitches on each row— two on the center four stitches or one either side of a center stitch. Once the shaping pattern is established it is repeated until no stitches remain.

This block needs a bit of planning and so it gives the impression of providing less opportunity for experiment while it is being worked. However, it is ideal when you already have a square space which you want to fill because it can be worked off the edges of other blocks and the half completed block is a very useful shape for garment shaping.

A half block can be created by positioning half the decrease stitches on one edge.

▼ **Single crochet mitered block**
This block has stripes but simple stitch patterns, beads, and loop stitches can all be added to the fabric as long as the shaping is maintained. The fabric drapes from the center decreases.

Tip If a stitch pattern is slightly wider than a single crochet fabric then occasionally work two extra decreases; one either side of the center of the block, to compensate.

Colorful stitch patterns

Jacquard patterns are where two or more colors are held in the hand and worked along a row from a chart, usually in single crochet. The colors are swapped and used as required. This type of crochet creates a colorful, sturdy fabric, with a "woven" look to it. Colorful stitch patterns in crochet can also use a variety of other techniques to introduce color into another row or make a color block appear as if it is worked over several dual colored rows.

Jacquard patterns

Jacquard patterns are worked from charts and usually only one repeat is shown. The chart shows the pattern as it will appear from the right side of the work and the odd-numbered rows are read from right to left and even-numbered rows from left to right. Begin by working the foundation chain in the first color at the bottom right of the chart. Calculate the number of chains to make according to the number of times you intend to repeat the pattern, then add one chain for turning. On the first row, work the first stitch into the second chain from the hook, then work the rest of the row in single crochet. Each square represents one stitch.

When changing yarns, carry the yarn not in use loosely across the back of the work and pick it up again when it is needed. This is called

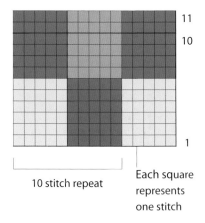

10 stitch repeat

Each square represents one stitch

stranding and it works well when the areas of color are narrow. To change colors, work until the last single crochet stitch of the first color, work the stitch but omit the last stage, leaving two loops on the hook. Complete the stitch with the second color. This is repeated as necessary

▲ Vertical stripes

Only one color was used at any one time but the same row was worked twice. First all one color was worked along the row with a chain loop between each block then the second color was worked in the same way along the same row. (See page 144 for pattern.)

▲ Horizontal stripes

Crochet rows need not be straight so it is easy with crochet stitches to create the impression of more than one color in a straight row but each stripe is two rows of single color blocks. (See page 136 for pattern).

along the row. The loose strands are prone to snagging and Jacquard is not reversible although the long strands of yarn do have a charm if they are regular and even.

Colorful stitch combinations

It is easier to achieve the appearance of more than one color in a row in crochet than knitting because stitches can be placed around or through lower stitches, the height of stitches can be varied, and by working back along small groups of stitches

elaborate blocks of color can be created. A hook can be removed from the working loop of crochet, the loop extended to prevent the accidental pulling of the stitch, and crochet stitches can be worked elsewhere on the piece or along part of the edge just worked. Then the abandoned loop can be picked up and work can continue over the new piece of crochet or elsewhere. In addition, this type of freeform work makes complex shaping possible. It is far easier using crochet because each stitch finishes with a single loop.

Intarsia patterns

Intarsia crochet produces a design that is reversible. Single crochet is usually used because it produces a dense stitch which helps give the color shapes definition and also because it is square and so there is a wealth of designs to choose from. Cross stitch designs are a good source of inspiration although they often need to be simplified but a knitting design would have to be redrawn because the knit stitch is not square.

▲ Blocks of color

If this block was pieced with an identical block, a diamond pattern would appear. If the block was pieced with an identical block but the corner of one was joined halfway up the edge of another, a zigzag pattern would be visible. (See page 151 for pattern.)

The main difference between the intarsia and Jacquard patterns is that, in intarsia, the color areas are larger and so colors not in use can't be carried across the back of the work. Instead, each color area is worked using a separate ball of yarn. The block to the left uses only three strands of color—one for each block of color. If the design was rotated and the yellow block was at the base then two strands of brown yarn would be required—one either side of the yellow block.

To work blocks of color while working in the round, change the colors as described but then with the new color insert the hook into the next stitch around the working strand of the last color, concealing it in the stitches of the new color. Continue in this way until the stitch before it will be required on the next round.

Working an intarsia pattern

1 Make the required length of foundation chain plus one stitch for the turning chain in yarn A , turn and work any plain rows at the bottom of the chart in single crochet. Work the first multicolored row, beginning with yarn A. At the color changes omit the last stage of the stitch before the change, leaving two loops on the hook. Join the next yarn by drawing a loop of the new color through the two loops. This completes the last stitch worked in the first yarn. Continue in the same way along the row.

2 When you reach the next color change in the row, in this case back to yarn A, work with another ball of the same yarn, not the one you used to begin the row.

Tip Take extra care when dealing with all the yarn ends on a piece of intarsia. Carefully darn each end into an area of crochet worked in the same color so it won't be visible on the right side.

3 At the end of the row, turn and work from the chart in the opposite direction, from left to right. At each color change, bring the old color forward and take the new one to the back ready to complete the stitch partially worked in the old color, making sure that you loop the new yarn round the old one on the wrong side of the work to prevent holes. At the end of wrong-side rows, make sure that all the yarns are back in the right place on the wrong side of the work.

Lace crochet

Cheaper than bobbin lace, fine crochet lace has long been used in lightweight shawls and decorative table linens. There are two types of lace: mesh patterns that tend to form a light background texture and are the basis of filet crochet and openwork which is more decorative. Both rely on contrast with areas of solid or grouped stitches to be decorative. A crochet lace without this contrast is a net and relies on its surroundings to add interest.

Foundation chains

Simple lace stitch patterns are very easy to work, but you should pay special attention to working the correct number of stitches in the foundation chain. For example, if foundation chain for a pattern requires a multiple of 2 stitches, so your chain must contain a number of stitches which is divisible by 2.

Some patterns require a multiple of chains, plus a few extra ones which are necessary for the pattern to be centered or repeat properly. Others will give you the multiple plus any extra stitches plus any chain required to reach the correct height for the first stitch. This information is often bracketed and may read, add 1 for base chain or foundation chain.

Working a trellis pattern

Similar in construction to mesh patterns, the chain spaces in trellis patterns are longer, allowing them to curve upward to create delicate arch-shaped loops. The chain spaces are usually anchored by single crochet stitches worked into the space below each loop.

Working a simple mesh pattern

1 Work the double crochet stitches of simple mesh patterns by inserting the hook into the chain space on the previous row and working the stitch as usual. Don't insert the hook into the chain stitch, but into the space below it.

2 Work the last double crochet stitch of each row into the third stitch of the turning chain. This makes a neater, firmer edge than working the stitch into the chain space.

Shells and lace
In crochet, lace holes are formed by chains, skipped stitches, and stitches of varying heights. Shells in lace patterns are popular because the contrast between the solid areas and the lighter areas to either side are a natural component of a shell group of stitches.

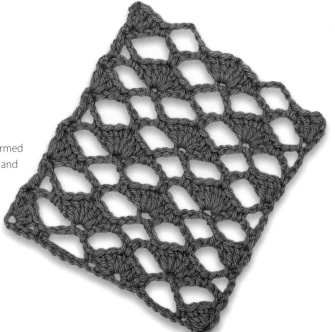

Filet crochet

Filet crochet is characterized by a mesh background on which the pattern is picked out in solid blocks of stitches. The open mesh should appear square. It is always worked from a chart, showing the pattern as it will appear from the right side of the work. The charts are numbered from side to side, reading odd-numbered rows from right to left and even-numbered rows from left to right. Choose a smooth yarn for a crisp appearance.

Each open square on a filet crochet chart represents one space or mesh—usually a space is made by working two double crochet stitches separated by two chains. When a square on the chart is filled in or has a dot or cross in the center, the chains are usually replaced by two double crochet stitches to make a solid block or mesh of four stitches. Two blocks together on the chart are filled by seven double crochet stitches, three blocks by ten stitches, and so on.

To calculate the number of stitches to make for the foundation chain at this gauge, you will need to multiply the number of squares across the chart by 3 and add 1. You will also need to add the correct number of turning chains, depending on whether the first chart row begins with a space or a block (see right).

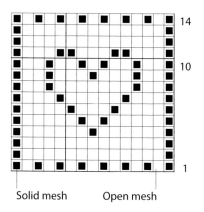

Solid mesh   Open mesh

The mesh size is not standard. Check the mesh size with each pattern because variations may have been used to achieve the fit required. Another popular mesh size has a open mesh of only one chain and this chain is replaced by one double crochet stitch for a solid mesh. This variation is useful if your gauge produces an open mesh which is a bit wide.

Working the first row

Make the foundation chain as described left or use a approximate foundation chain (see page 113). Start to follow the chart from the bottom right-hand corner, along the row of squares marked 1.

Starting the first row with a space

When the first square is a space, add 4 turning chains and work the first double crochet stitch into the 8th chain from the hook. Continue working spaces and blocks along the row, reading the chart from right to left.

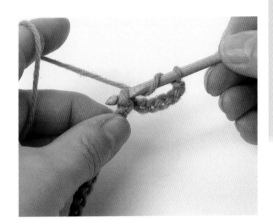

Starting the first row with a block

1 When the first square on the chart is a block, add 2 turning chains and work the first double crochet stitch into the 4th chain from the hook.

2 Work 1 double crochet stitch into each of the next 2 chains to complete the block. Continue along the row, reading the chart from right to left.

Working the rest of the chart rows

At the end of the first row, turn the work and follow the second row of the chart, reading from left to right. Work spaces and blocks at the beginning and end of the second and subsequent rows as follows.

Working a space over a space on the previous row

At the beginning of a row, work 5 turning ch (counts as 1 dc and 2 ch), skip the first stitch and the next 2 ch, work 1 dc into the next dc, then continue working from the chart.

At the end of a row, finish with 1 dc into the last dc, work 2 ch, skip 2 ch, work 1 dc into the third ch of 5 turning chains, turn.

Working a space over a block on the previous row

At the beginning of the row, work 5 turning ch (counts as 1 dc and 2 ch), skip the first 3 stitches, work 1 dc into the next dc, then continue working spaces and blocks from the chart.

At the end of a row, work to the last 4 stitches. Work 1 dc into the next stitch, work 2 ch, skip 2 stitches, work 1 dc into the top ch of 3 turning chains to complete the block, turn.

Working a block over a space on the previous row

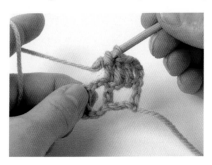 

At the beginning of the row, work
3 turning ch (counts as 1 dc), skip 1 stitch,
work 1 dc into each of the next 2 ch, 1 dc
into the next stitch to complete the block.
Continue across the row working spaces
and blocks from the chart.

At the end of a row, finish with 1 dc into
the last dc, 1 dc into each of the next 3 ch
of the turning chain, turn.

Working a block over a block on the previous row

At the beginning of the row, work
3 turning ch (counts as 1 dc), skip 1 stitch,
work 1 dc into each of the next 3 dc to
complete the block. Continue across
the row working spaces and blocks
from the chart.

At the end of a row, finish with 1 dc into
each of the last 3 dc, 1 dc stitch into the
top ch of 3 turning chains, turn.

Shaping filet and lace crochet

The shaping is demonstrated on filet lace. However, these techniques are also useful for lace crochet not based on a mesh. The shaping is carried out at the beginning and end of the row and makes neat sloping edges to shape sleeves and necklines or unusually shaped table linens. It is sometimes useful to try and adjust your working gauge slightly so that it is slacker than usual for increases and tighter than usual for decreases.

Slanted increase

This method uses extra chain stitches or a slightly longer additional stitch to slant away from the fabric edge. The stitch and chain heights can be adjusted to ensure a smooth slanted increase.

Increasing with an open mesh at the beginning of the row

Make 6 turning ch (counts as 1 tr and 2 chains). Work 1 dc in the same place, then continue along the row.

Increasing with an open mesh at the end of the row

Work 2 ch, then 1 tr into the top of the turning chain on the previous row.

Slanted decrease

This method uses slightly longer additional stitches or the equivalent chain to span a mesh block at a diagonal. The stitch and chain heights can be adjusted to ensure a smooth slanted increase.

Decreasing with an open mesh at the beginning of the row

Work 4 turning ch (counts as 1 tr), skip the next block or space, work 1 dc into the first stitch of the next space or block.

Decreasing with an open mesh at the end of the row

1 Work an incomplete dc into the first stitch of the last space or block, leaving 2 loops on the hook. Yarn over hook twice (ready to make a treble stitch), insert hook into the top of the turning chain on the previous row.

2 Yarn over hook, pull through one loop on the hook (5 loops on hook), yarn over hook, pull through the first 2 loops on the hook (4 loops on hook).

3 Yarn over hook, pull through 2 loops on hook (3 loops on hook), yarn over hook, pull through the remaining 3 loops to complete the decrease.

Hairpin crochet

Hairpin crochet (also called hairpin lace and hairpin braid) is worked with an ordinary crochet hook and a special hairpin tool. It is the perfect technique for showcasing beautiful hand-dyed and spun yarns but the large loops can be prone to snagging. The technique makes strips of very lacy crochet, which are often used to decorate the edges of ordinary crochet or pieced together to make large, airy shawls or afghans.

Hairpin tools are adjustable, so you can make different widths of crochet. The metal pins are held in position by clips or bars at the top and bottom, and they can be placed close together to make a narrow strip or moved further apart to make wide strips.

A series of loops are made between the two pins using the yarn and the crochet hook until the tool is full of loops. At this point, the loops are taken off the pins, leaving the final few loops attached so that work can continue. When the strip reaches the desired length, all the loops are taken off the tool. You can use the hairpin crochet exactly as it comes off the tool, or you can work a row of single crochet along each looped edge if you prefer.

Working hairpin lace foundation stitches

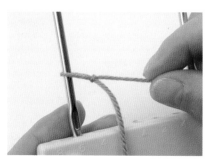

1 Arrange the pins in the bottom clip so they are the required distance apart. Make a slip knot in the yarn and loop it over the left-hand pin.

2 Ease the knot across so it lies in the center between the pins. Take the yarn back around the right-hand pin, tensioning it between your fingers as if you were working ordinary crochet.

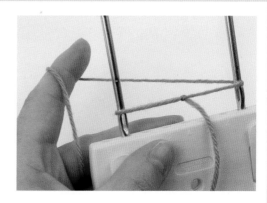

3 Insert the crochet hook into the loop on the left-hand pin, wrap the yarn over the hook, and draw it through the loop.

4 Wrap the yarn over the hook again and draw it through the loop on the hook to secure the yarn.

Tip If you find it difficult to keep the work centered between the pins, secure the yarn end to the clip with a piece of masking tape after you've centered the knot.

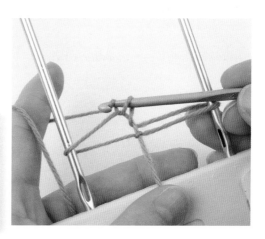

Working hairpin lace

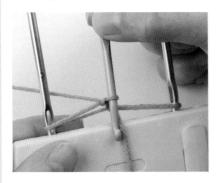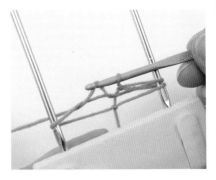

1 Holding the hook vertically, turn the hairpin tool 180º clockwise to make a half turn. The yarn is now wound round the right-hand pin and the other side of the clip is facing you.

2 Insert the hook under the front loop on the left-hand pin, pick up the yarn at the back of the tool, and draw a loop of yarn through so there are two loops on the hook.

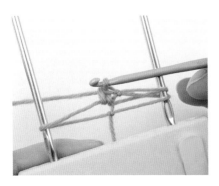

3 Wrap the yarn over the hook and draw through the two loops on the hook to make a single crochet stitch.

4 Repeat steps 1, 2, and 3 until the hairpin tool is filled with braid, remembering to turn the tool clockwise each time.

Working when the hairpin tool is full

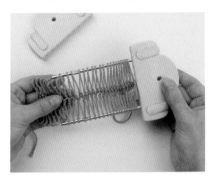

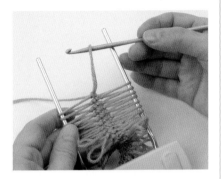

1 When the tool is full, put the top clip onto the pins, remove the lower clip, and slide the crochet strip downward, leaving the last few loops on the pins.

2 Reinsert the lower clip, remove the top clip, and continue working the strip as above. When the strip is the required length, pull the yarn end through the last stitch with the hook, and slide the strip off the pins.

Working an edging to the hairpin lace

To work an edging, make a slip knot on the hook, insert the hook into the first loop along one edge, and work a single crochet stitch. Keeping the loops twisted in the same way they came off the pins, work a single crochet into each loop along the edge, then fasten off the yarn. Repeat along the second edge.

Broomstick crochet

Broomstick crochet is worked with an ordinary crochet hook and a large knitting needle, and makes a soft, very lacy fabric. The length of the knitting needle determines the width of the crochet fabric, so you may need to make several strips and sew them together to get the desired width. This technique is used to make shawls, scarves, wraps, and blankets, and it looks good worked in a smooth woolen yarn or a soft mohair.

Working broomstick crochet

Each row of broomstick crochet is worked in two stages. In the first stage, the loop row, a series of loops are worked and transferred onto the needle. On the return row, all the loops are slipped off the needle, then crocheted together to make groups. For the beginner, it's best to make a two-row foundation as shown below, but the more experienced crocheter can work the first row directly into a foundation chain.

Working a foundation row for broomstick crochet

Make a foundation chain to the width required, making sure you have a multiple of five stitches plus turning chain, then turn and work a row of single crochet into the chain.

Working the loop row for broomstick crochet

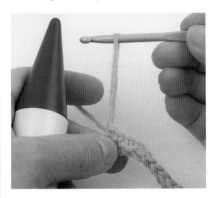

1 Hold the knitting needle securely under your left arm, extend the loop already on the crochet hook, and slip it over the needle.

2 Insert the hook into the second stitch, wrap the yarn and draw a loop through, then extend the loop and slip it onto the needle.

3 Draw a loop through each stitch of the foundation row in the same way to finish the loop row. Check that the number of loops is a multiple of five.

Tip You may find that broomstick crochet is rather awkward to work at first, especially when working the loop rows. Gripping the knitting needle between your knees instead of holding it under your arm can help.

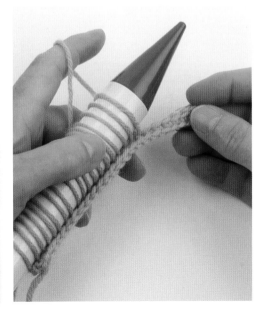

Working the return row for broomstick crochet

1 Slip all the loops off the needle and hold the work in your left hand. Insert the hook from right to left through the first five loops.

2 Wrap the yarn and draw a loop through the center of the five-loop group and make one chain.

3 Work five single crochet stitches through the center of the loops. Continue along the row of loops in the same way, grouping five loops together, and working five single crochet stitches through the center of the loops to complete the first return row.

4 To work the next loop row, do not turn the work. Extend the first loop over the needle as before, and repeat the loop row as above. Continue working alternate loop and return rows until the fabric is the required length, ending with a return row.

▲ **Which side is the right side?**
Use either the smooth side (above right) or the ridged side (left) as the right side of your broomstick crochet.

Tunisian crochet

Tunisian crochet combines the techniques of both crochet and knitting, and produces a strong, elastic fabric. Tunisian crochet hooks look like long knitting needles with a hook at one end, and they are available in the same range of sizes as standard crochet hooks and varying lengths. A standard crochet hook with a throat plate cannot be used for Tunisian crochet. The fabric is usually worked to be thick and dense and it is very hard wearing.

Tunisian crochet fabric

Tunisian crochet fabric is made on a foundation chain, and each row is worked in two stages. In the first stage, the loop row, a series of loops are made onto the needle, then on the return row the loops are worked off the needle in pairs without turning the work. Plain Tunisian stitch (below) is the simplest stitch. Other stitches are variations and are made by inserting the hook in different positions, and changing how the loops are worked. Yarn and hook are held in the same way as for ordinary crochet.

Working a foundation row of plain Tunisian stitch

1 Make a crochet foundation chain in the usual way. Insert the hook into the back loop of the second chain, wrap the yarn over the hook and draw a loop through the chain so you have two loops on the hook.

2 Insert the hook into the back loop of the third chain, wrap the yarn over the hook, and draw a loop through so you have three loops on the hook.

3 Repeat along the row until you have made a loop from each chain and have a row of loops on the hook. Do not turn the work.

Working a return row on the foundation row of plain Tunisian stitch

Wrap the yarn over the hook and draw it through the first loop on the hook. Wrap the yarn over the hook and draw it through the next two loops on the hook. Continue working from left to right, working off two loops at a time until you have only one loop left on the hook.

Working the second loop row of plain Tunisian stitch

1 Skip the first vertical bar, and insert the hook from right to left under the next vertical bar, wrap the yarn over the hook and draw through to make a loop on the hook so you have two loops on the hook.

2 Insert the hook under the next vertical bar, wrap the yarn over the hook, and draw a loop through so you have three loops on the hook. Repeat along the row until you have a row of loops on the hook. Do not turn the work.

Working the return row of plain Tunisian stitch

Wrap the yarn over the hook, and draw it through the first loop on the hook, then work off the row of loops in the same way as the loop row above, leaving one loop on the hook at the end of the row. Repeat from working a loop row and then a return row for length required, ending with a return row.

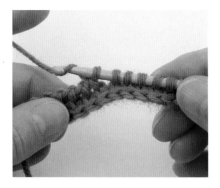

The top edge of Tunisian crochet

After working a piece of Tunisian crochet, finish off the top edge with a row of single crochet to neaten and strengthen the edge.

Finishing the top edge of Tunisian crochet

1 Wrap the yarn over the hook and draw it through the first loop on the hook to make a chain.

2 Insert the hook from right to left under the second vertical bar, wrap the yarn round the hook and draw a loop through so you have two loops on the hook.

3 Wrap the yarn over the hook again and draw it through both loops on the hook to complete the single crochet.

4 Work a single crochet under each vertical bar of the row, then fasten off the yarn.

Finishing Techniques

Finishing Techniques

Blocking

The first stage of finishing—blocking—involves easing and pinning the crocheted pieces into the correct shape, then either steaming with an iron or moistening with cold water depending on the fiber content of your yarn. Always be guided by the information given on the ball band of your yarn (see pages 12–13 for details of different yarns and fibers) and, when in doubt, choose the cold-water blocking method (opposite).

Yarns made from most natural fibers (cotton, linen, wool, but not silk, which is more delicate) can be blocked with warm steam. A large item such as an afghan made in one piece (or from motifs which have been joined together as you go) can be carefully pressed from the wrong side over a well-padded ironing board, using a light touch to avoid crushing the stitches. Never, ever, attempt to steam or press

Tip Plastic-headed or pearl-beaded pins can be used for pinning crochet and for cold-water blocking, but don't use this type for warm-steam blocking as the heat of the iron will melt the plastic heads.

a crochet piece made from man-made yarns such as nylon or acrylic—you will probably melt the yarn, or at the very least flatten it and make it limp and lifeless. Instead, use the cold-water blocking method shown here.

To block garment pieces and separate motifs, it's a good idea to make your own blocking board. You can do this inexpensively by covering a piece of flat board with one or two layers of quilter's batting and then a layer of fabric. Choose a cotton check fabric so it can withstand the heat of the iron and help you pin out straight edges. Use plenty of rustproof glass-headed pins to pin out the pieces. When pinning out long pieces such as edgings, work in sections and allow each section to dry before moving on to the next one.

Blocking with warm steam

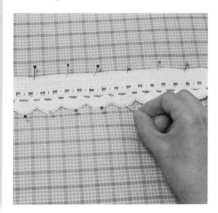

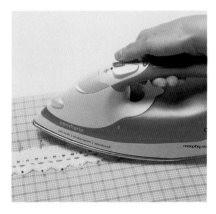

1 Pin out the crochet piece, using the checks on the fabric to help you keep the edges straight. Be generous with the number of pins you use and gently ease the crochet into shape before inserting each pin. Unless the piece is heavily textured and needs to be blocked face-up, you can block crochet with either the right or wrong side facing upward.

2 To block natural fiber yarns with warm steam, hold a steam iron set at the correct temperature for the yarn about ¾ in. (2 cm) above the surface of the crochet and allow the steam to penetrate for several seconds. Work in sections and don't allow the iron to come into contact with the crochet surface. Allow the crochet to dry before removing the pins.

Blocking with cold water

Pin out the pieces as above, then use a spray bottle to mist the crochet with clean cold water until it is evenly moist all over, but not saturated. When blocking heavyweight yarns, gently pat the crochet with your hand to help the moisture penetrate more easily. Lay the board flat and allow the crochet to dry before removing the pins.

Sewn seams

A back-stitch seam is durable but rather bulky for lightweight garments, so use this method for seaming loose-fitting garments such as winter sweaters. A woven seam gives a flatter finish as the pieces are joined edge to edge. This method works better when finishing fine work and baby garments. Use the same yarn for both the crochet fabric and seams, unless your yarn is thick or textured, in which case use a finer yarn of matching color.

Back-stitch seam

Place the pieces to be joined together with the right sides facing and pin, inserting the pins at right angles to the edge. Thread a large tapestry needle with yarn and work a row of back stitch from right to left, close to the edge.

Woven seam

Place the pieces to be joined side by side on a flat surface with the wrong side facing upward and the edges touching. Thread a large tapestry needle with yarn and work a row of evenly spaced stitches in a loose zigzag pattern from edge to edge, carefully tightening the gauge of the stitches as you work so the edges pull together.

Sewing through the back loops

1 Lay out the motifs to be joined in the correct order with the right side of each motif facing up. Working first in horizontal rows, overcast the motifs together. Begin stitching at the right-hand edge of the first two motifs, inserting the needle into the back loop of corresponding stitches.

2 Continue overcasting the first two motifs together until you reach the left-hand corner. Align the next two motifs, carry the thread firmly across and join them together in the same way. Continue joining motifs along the row, then secure the thread carefully at the beginning and end of the stitching. Repeat until all the horizontal edges of the motifs are joined.

3 Turn the work so the remaining edges of the motifs are now horizontal. Work in the same way as above. When working the corners, take the needle under the stitch made on the previous row.

Tip To make a stronger but slightly less neat join than the one shown above, work in the same way, but insert the needle through both loops of the motif edges.

Crochet seams

Motifs can be joined, either by sewing them together, or with rows of slip stitch or single crochet. Take particular care with the gauge of the crochet seam stitch—a slightly looser gauge would allow the seam to stretch but it isn't always possible to use a larger hook. Use matching yarn when joining with crochet, although you can make a decorative statement when using slip stitch by choosing a contrasting color of yarn.

Joining with slip stitch

1 Place the first two motifs together, wrong sides facing, and work a row of slip stitch (page 19) through both loops of each motif. When you reach the corner, align the next two motifs, carry the thread firmly across and join them together in the same way. Continue joining motifs along the row, keeping your gauge even. Repeat until all the horizontal edges of the motifs are joined.

2 Turn the work so the remaining edges of the motifs are now horizontal. Working in the same way as above, join the remaining edges together with horizontal rows of slip stitch. When working the corners, carry the thread firmly across the ridge.

Joining with single crochet through both loops

Single crochet (page 20) can also be used to join edges together, but it makes a thick seam which looks neatest when the stitches are worked on the wrong side of the work. Seam the motifs in the same order as for slip stitch joins (left), but place the motifs right sides together and work rows of single crochet through both loops of the motif edges.

Joining with single crochet through the back loop only

To make a less heavy and more elastic single crochet seam, place the motifs right sides together and work the rows of single crochet stitches through the back loops only.

Tip If you're finding it difficult inserting your hook through the edges of the squares, use a metal hook or one which has a more pointed tip.

Button loops and buttonholes

Bands with buttons, buttonholes, and loops are best worked in single crochet for strength and neatness. Button loops are a decorative alternative to the ordinary buttonhole, especially for lacy garments. Make the button band first. Mark the positions of the buttons with safety pins and work the buttonhole (or button loop) band to match, making holes or loops opposite the safety pin markers.

Working button loops

1 Work a row of evenly spaced single crochet along the garment edge, with the right side of the garment facing you. Work in single crochet to the position of the loop, skip two or three stitches and work a loop of chains to accommodate the button. Continue in the same way until all the loops have been worked.

2 On the next row, reinforce the loops by working a slip stitch into each stitch and each chain along the row.

Working buttonholes

1 Work a row of evenly spaced single crochet along the garment edge, with the right side of the garment facing you. Work additional rows of single crochet until the band is the required width for positioning the buttonholes, usually half the total width.

2 Work in single crochet to the position of the buttonhole, skip a few stitches to accommodate the size of the button, and work the same number of chains over the skipped stitches. Continue in the same way until all the holes have been worked.

3 On the next row, work a single crochet into each stitch and each chain along the row. Work additional rows of single crochet until the buttonhole band is the same width as the button band.

Buttons and zippers

Buttons add style to any crochet garment. They may be purely functional or form one of the main design features. Crochet button designs are widely available and enable buttons to be coordinated with the project. Beaded crochet button designs are particularly effective. Zippers offer a strong fastening for projects that have very little ease and would be likely to gape if buttons or hooks and eyes were used.

Making a ball button

1 Work a ball button over a bead or a small ball of stuffing. Using a smaller hook than suggested for the yarn you are using, ch 2, then work 4 sc into the first ch. Without joining or turning the work, work 2 sc into each stitch made on the previous round. For the next and every following increase round, work * 1 sc in first st, 2 sc into next stitch; repeat from * until the piece covers one half of the bead or ball of stuffing. Slip the bead or ball into the cover. Start decreasing by working * 1 sc into next st, sc2tog; repeat from * until the bead or ball is completely covered.

2 Break off the yarn, leaving an end of about 12 in. (30 cm). Thread the yarn into a large tapestry needle and work a few stitches to secure.

Inserting a zipper into a seam

1 Sew the seam leaving an opening long enough to accommodate the zipper from pull to just above the end stop. Pin the zipper into position making sure the crochet stitch pattern matches on either side of the zipper opening.

2 Using matching sewing thread and small running stitches, sew the zipper tapes to the crochet fabric.

Inserting a separating zipper

Work a row of single crochet edging along each edge. Pin the zipper in place with the single crochet edge lining up just beyond the outer edge of the teeth. Turn under the tapes at the top and bottom. Pull the zipper to check it runs smoothly, and sew in place as above.

Tidying the zipper back

This gives the zipper extra strength and stops the tape being snagged. On the wrong side, carefully stitch the tape onto the back of the crochet fabric using small, evenly spaced stitches and taking care to stitch into the back of the crochet stitches, not through to the front of the crochet piece.

Surface embellishment

The joy of surface embellishment is that it provides the perfect opportunity to add those little details that will make a project special. Techniques such as surface crochet, appliqué, weaving, and embroidery are best done when the project is blocked and seamed and can be seen as a whole for the first time. Of course all these things should be planned from the start but it is all right to plan to decide at the end of a project too.

▲ Surface crochet
Working surface crochet with contrasting yarn textures is particularly effective.

Once a project has been completed it is often useful to take the time to really look at it and live with it for a while. One way to do this is to display it where you will see it every day or can quickly try it on if it is a garment for you. This is an opportunity to decide whether or not the attention of the viewer will be in the right places or if an extra detail will just add that little sparkle. Twist and pin anything of the right texture, weight, and color to the project to map out a design.

Surface crochet

Surface crochet is exactly as the name suggests, crochet worked on top of a background fabric. You can work on plain single crochet fabric, but the lines of surface slip stitch also look effective worked on a mesh background. If you can, choose a smooth yarn to make the background, then you can add rows of contrasting colors and textures to the surface using this technique.

Holding the contrast yarn behind the crochet fabric, simply insert the hook through the fabric, and draw a loop of yarn through to make a slip stitch. Continue in this way, creating a chain stitch sitting on the surface of the fabric.

Woven crochet

Open crochet stitches may be used as a basis for woven crochet. After making a piece of crochet fabric in a simple stitch, contrasting yarns are woven through the holes with a tapestry needle. If the piece is going to require regular laundry consider carefully the fiber content of the yarns. If in doubt, match the fiber to the background crochet. The woven threads can be worked in any direction or even randomly.

Tip Prepare the surface to be embellished by either blocking it or, in the case of woven fabric, pressing it. Consider using an embroidery frame for larger embroideries.

Appliqué flower
Even a simple crochet flower motif can add a focal point. For pattern see page 166.

Appliqué

Appliqué is the attaching of separate motifs to a fabric. Crochet is perfect for both the motifs and the background fabric because a strong dense fabric can be created to either create the motif or support it. The motifs are usually sewn on using matching sewing thread and small running stitches but they can also be attached using surface crochet. For a contrast, fabric motifs also work well on a crochet background.

Finishing edges

An edge finish differs from a crochet edging or border (pages 112–113) in the method of working. An edge finish is worked directly into the crochet fabric, unlike an edging or border which is worked separately, then stitched onto crochet or woven fabric as a decoration. A finishing edge is often used to add strength or stability to an edge or to give it a attractive finish.

Single crochet edging is the most popular and is used mainly for finishing necklines and borders on garments. Single crochet is also very effective worked in a contrasting color of yarn. Reverse single crochet stitch edging is more hardwearing due to the small knots of yarn made along the row. It can be worked directly into the edge (as shown right) or several rows of single crochet can be worked first to act as a foundation. Picot and shell edgings offer a more decorative finish.

Whatever the choice of stitch, work a sample on the gauge swatch. If a different yarn and gauge is being used calculate the gauge of the new edge stitches—the ideal spacing along the edge—and find a rhythm of stitches that will space them evenly along the edge and make the finishing edge look neat.

Working a single crochet edging

Single crochet is a useful and flexible but not elastic edge finish. Working from right to left, make a row of ordinary single crochet stitches (pages 20) into the edge of the crochet fabric, spacing the stitches evenly along the edge.

Reverse single crochet edging

Also known as crab stitch, this stitch makes a strong, fairly rigid edging with an attractive texture. Unlike most other crochet techniques, this stitch is worked from left to right along the row.

Working a reverse single crochet edging

1 Keeping the yarn to the left, insert the hook from front to back into the next stitch and wind the yarn over the hook.

2 Draw the loop through from back to front so there are now two loops on the hook. Yarn over hook, then draw the yarn through both loops to complete the stitch.

A picot edge

This stitch makes a delicate edge with tiny protruding loops of yarn.

Working a picot edge

Work a foundation row of single crochet and turn. * Work ch 3, slip stitch into 3rd chain from hook (one picot made). Skip 1 stitch, then work a slip stitch into the next stitch. Repeat from * along the edge.

Edgings, braids, and insertions

Edgings, braids, and insertions are strips of crochet, which can be stitched to pieces of crochet or woven fabrics to decorate the edges or join two edges. An edging usually has one straight edge and one fancy edge, a braid can have two fancy edges, and an insertion usually has two straight edges. Having said that, these definitions vary from publication to publication and they are all usually simply described as edgings or trimmings.

Depending on the pattern, edgings can be worked in short rows across the width or in long rows across the length. Most edgings can be made deeper by working a straight band of crochet. This is called a header and is usually worked in single crochet.

On edgings worked widthwise, extra stitches are added to the foundation chain and each time that edge is reached extra stitches are worked. Headers are usually plain but a regular band of holes can be used to hold a ribbon or a few beads can be added to not only add sparkle to an edge but weight which may be used to improve the drape.

Edgings worked widthwise

Many braids are worked widthwise on a small number of stitches. The advantage of selecting an edging worked widthwise is that it is easier to adjust the length.

Working a braid widthwise

Keep turning the braid and repeating the pattern row until it is the required length, then fasten off the yarn.

Edgings worked lengthwise

All manner of edgings are worked lengthwise from shell patterns and lace to chain fringes and raised stitch ribs. The advantage of selecting an edging worked lengthwise is that it is easier to adjust the depth of the edging and even add a few rows at a later date. To ensure that the correct number of stitches is worked in the foundation chain for the length, use an approximate foundation

Braids ▶

Braid patterns are usually worked lengthwise from a foundation, then extra rows of crochet are worked along the two long edges.

chain. This method works very well as long as care is taken not to stretch the foundation chain too much. The finished edging may not be as elastic.

Making an approximate foundation chain

Make a foundation chain about 25 stitches longer than the pattern states. Work the first pattern row along the chain in the usual way, checking the length of your work against the edge you wish to decorate. When crochet and edge match in length (and you have the correct multiple of stitches to work the pattern), turn and work the second row, leaving the extra chains unworked. When the edging or border is complete, snip off the slip knot at the end of the chain with a sharp pair of scissors. Using a tapestry needle, unpick the first one or two chain stitches until the chains will slip through each other when the yarn end is pulled. Unravel the chain up to the edge of the crochet, then weave the yarn end in the usual way.

Attaching edgings

To attach edgings, braids, and insertions, hand stitch a braid to fabric using tiny stitches down the center or along each edge with matching sewing thread. Providing the glue is compatible with the fiber composition of the yarn, use a glue gun to attach braid to a box or basket.

Fringes and tassels

Fringes and tassels can look very effective attached to the edge of an afghan, cushion, bag, or even garment. They add some weight so improve poor drape, but they also add movement to a crochet project. Fringes and tassels can use up a lot of yarn. One solution, should you fear you haven't got enough yarn, is to mix several yarns together. If slightly darker colors are mixed in, it will make the fringe or tassels look thicker.

Crochet fringes

As a change from the usual yarn fringe of the type found on scarves, try making a crochet fringe. A chain fringe is made from loops of crochet chain; a corkscrew fringe is made from strips of single crochet worked so they curl round and round. They are easily adapted—vary the length of the chain and frequency of the fringe as required.

Making a chain fringe

On the fringe row, chain 15 and join the end of the chain with a slip stitch into the same place as the previous single crochet stitch. Vary the length of the chain and its frequency as required.

Making a corkscrew fringe

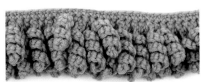

To make the corkscrew shapes, chain 15 and turn. Work two single crochet stitches into the 2nd chain from the hook and into each remaining chain.

Making a fringe tassel

1 Decide how deep the finished fringe will be and cut a rectangle of stiff cardboard to the same depth plus ½ in. (1 cm) to allow for trimming. Wind yarn evenly around the cardboard, cut along the bottom edge to make strands. Repeat until you have the required number of strands.

2 Mark the position of each fringe tassel on the right side of the crochet edge with pins. Insert a large hook from front to back through the crochet. Gather the required number of yarn strands into a neat group, fold in half, and loop the fold over the hook.

3 Carefully pull the hook and the folded yarn strands through the crochet for a short distance.

4 Loop the hook around the cut ends of the yarn group and pull gently through to complete the tassel. Repeat until the fringe is complete, then carefully trim the cut ends with a sharp pair of scissors.

Cords

Crochet cords can be used as straps for purses, ties to secure a neckline, or they can be sewn onto a plain piece of crochet to decorate it with shapes such as spirals, stripes, or swirls. Use a crochet spiral to trim a key ring or the tab on a zipper. You can make a large cluster of them to decorate each corner of an afghan as a novel alternative to a tassel. Experiment with different yarn textures and colors and beads to increase the possibilities further.

Crochet cords can be made in several different ways. They can be flat or rounded, narrow, or generously wide. When making a crochet cord, you'll need to make the foundation chain longer than the finished cord you require, because the chain will contract as you work into it.

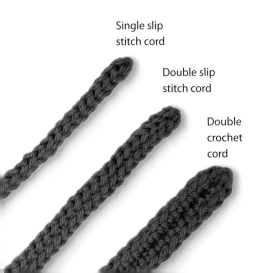

Single slip stitch cord

Double slip stitch cord

Double crochet cord

Making a single slip stitch cord

Work a foundation chain to the required length. Change to a size smaller hook, insert into the second chain from the hook and work a row of slip stitch along one side of the chain.

Tip For a double slip stitch cord, work as for a single slip stitch cord, then chain 1, and slip stitch along the other edge.

Making a single crochet cord

1 Work a foundation chain to the required length. Change to a size smaller hook, insert into the second chain from the hook and work a row of single crochet stitches along one side of the chain.

2 At the end of the first side, ch 1, turn, and work along the second side of the chain in the same way.

Making a plain spiral cord

2 Fasten off the yarn at the end of the row, leaving a yarn end of about 12 in. (30 cm) to attach the spiral.

1 Work a loose foundation chain of 30 stitches. Change to a size smaller hook and work two double crochet stitches into the fourth chain from the hook. Continue along the chain working four double crochet stitches into each chain. As you work, the crochet will begin to twist into a spiral formation naturally.

Making a striped spiral

Using yarn A, work a plain spiral as above and fasten off. Join yarn B, work a row of single crochet stitches along the edge, and fasten off.

Stitch and Block directory

Stitch and Block Directory

1

ch = chain,
see page 18.

sl st = slip stitch,
see page 19.

dc = double
crochet, see
page 24.

Abbreviations
and symbols,
see page 180.

Traditional granny

Note

Worked in 6 colors, A,
B, C, D, E, and F.

FOUNDATION RING: using yarn
A, ch 6 and join with sl st to form
a ring.

ROUND 1: ch 3 (counts as 1 dc),
2 dc into ring, ch 3, *3 dc into
ring, ch 3; rep from * twice more,
join with sl st into 3rd of 3-ch.
Break off yarn A. Join yarn B to
any 3-ch-sp.

ROUND 2: ch 3 (counts as 1 dc), [2 dc, ch 3, 3 dc] into same sp (corner made), *ch 1, [3 dc, ch 3, 3 dc] into next 3-ch-sp; rep from * twice more, ch 1, join with sl st into 3rd of 3-ch.
Break off yarn B. Join yarn C to any 3-ch-sp.

ROUND 3: ch 3 (counts as 1 dc), [2 dc, ch 3, 3 dc] into same sp, *ch 1, 3 dc into 1-ch-sp, ch 1, **[3 dc, ch 3, 3 dc] into next 3-ch-corner-sp; rep from * twice and from * to ** once again, join with sl st into 3rd of 3-ch.
Break off yarn C. Join yarn D to any 3-ch-corner-sp.

ROUND 4: ch 3 (counts as 1 dc), [2 dc, ch 3, 3 dc] into same sp, *[ch 1, 3 dc] into each 1-ch-sp along side of square, ch 1, **[3 dc, ch 3, 3 dc] into next 3-ch-corner-sp; rep from * twice and from * to ** once again, join with sl st into 3rd of 3-ch.
Break off yarn D. Join yarn E to any 3-ch-corner-sp.

ROUND 5: ch 3 (counts as 1 dc), [2 dc, ch 3, 3 dc] into same sp, *[ch 1, 3 dc] into each 1-ch-sp along side of square, ch 1, **[3 dc, ch 3, 3 dc] into next 3-ch-corner sp; rep from * twice and from * to ** once again, join with sl st into 3rd of 3-ch.
Break off yarn E. Join yarn F to any 3-ch-corner-sp.

ROUND 6: ch 3 (counts as 1 dc), [2 dc, ch 3, 3 dc] into same sp, *[ch 1, 3 dc] into each 1-ch-sp along side of square, ch 1, **[3 dc, ch 3, 3 dc] into next 3-ch-corner-sp; rep from * twice and from * to ** once again, join with sl st into 3rd of 3-ch.

ROUND 7: sl st in next 2 dc and into next 3-ch-corner-sp, ch 3 (counts as 1 dc), [2 dc, ch 3, 3 dc] into same sp, *[ch 1, 3 dc] into each 1-ch-sp along side of square, ch 1, **[3 dc, ch 3, 3 dc] into next 3-ch-corner-sp; rep from * twice and from * to ** once again, join with sl st into 3rd of 3-ch.
Fasten off yarn.

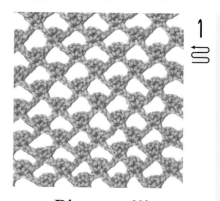

Picot trellis

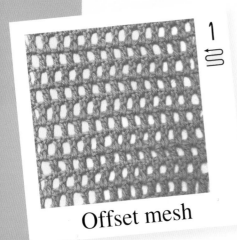

Offset mesh

ch = chain,
see page 18.

sc = single
crochet, see
page 20.

dc = double
crochet, see
page 24.

Abbreviations
and symbols,
see page 180.

🌀 **FOUNDATION CHAIN:**
multiple of 2.
Make the required length
of foundation chain.

FOUNDATION ROW (RS): 1 dc into
6th ch from hook, * ch 1, skip
1 ch, 1 dc into next ch; rep from *
ending with 1 dc into last ch, turn.

ROW 1: ch 4 (counts as 1 dc, ch 1),
1 dc into first 1-ch-sp, * ch 1, skip
1 dc, 1 dc into next 1-ch-sp; rep
from * to turning ch, 1 dc into
3rd ch of 4-ch, turn.

Rep row 1.

Fasten off yarn.

🌀 **FOUNDATION CHAIN:** multiple
of 5 chains plus 2.
Make the required length
of foundation chain.

FOUNDATION ROW: 1 sc into 2nd
ch from hook, * ch 5, skip 4 ch,
1 sc into next ch; rep from * to
end, turn.

ROW 1: * ch 5, work a picot of
[1 sc, ch 3, 1 sc] into 3rd ch of
next 5-ch-loop; rep from * ending
with ch 2, 1 dc into last sc, turn.

ROW 2: ch 1, 1 sc into first st,
* ch 5, skip picot, make picot into
3rd ch of next 5-ch-loop; rep from
* ending with ch 5, skip picot,
1 sc into arch made by turning
ch, turn.

Rep rows 1–2.

Fasten off yarn.

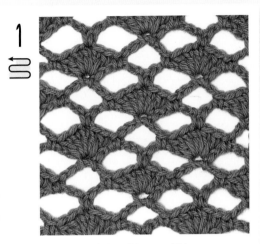

Shell trellis

FOUNDATION CHAIN: multiple of 12 chains plus 3.
Make the required length of foundation chain.
FOUNDATION ROW (RS): 2 dc into 3rd ch from hook, * skip 2 ch, 1 sc into next ch, ch 5, skip 5 ch, 1 sc into next ch, skip 2 ch, 5 dc into next ch; rep from * ending last rep with only 3 dc into last ch, turn.
ROW 1: ch 1, 1 sc into first st, *ch 5, 1 sc into next 5-ch-loop, ch 5, 1 sc into 3rd dc of next 5 dc; rep from * ending last rep with 1 sc into top of turning ch, turn.

ROW 2: * ch 5, 1 sc into next 5-ch-loop, 5 dc into next sc, 1 sc into next 5-ch-loop; rep from * ending with ch 2, 1 dc into last sc, turn.
ROW 3: ch 1, 1 sc into first st, * ch 5, 1 sc into 3rd dc of next 5 dc, ch 5, 1 sc into next 5-ch-loop; rep from * to end, turn.
ROW 4: ch 3 (counts as 1 dc), 2 dc into first st, * 1 sc into next 5-ch-loop, ch 5, 1 sc into next 5-ch-loop, 5 dc into next sc; rep from * ending last rep with only 3 dc into last sc, turn.
Rep rows 1–4.
Fasten off yarn.

ch = chain, see page 18.

sc = single crochet, see page 20.

dc = double crochet, see page 24.

Abbreviations and symbols, see page 180.

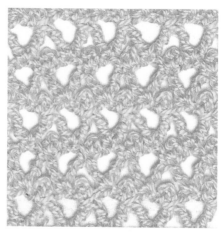

Picot triangles

ch = chain,
see page 18.

tr = treble
crochet, see
page 26.

tr2tog =
treble crochet
2 sts tog, see
page 39.

Abbreviations
and symbols,
see page 180.

FOUNDATION CHAIN: multiple of 4 chains plus 3.
Make the required length of foundation chain.
ROW 1: 1 tr in 5th ch from hook, *ch 3, tr2tog, inserting hook first in same ch as previous tr, then in following 4th ch, 1 picot; repeat from * to last 2-ch, ch 3, tr2tog, inserting hook first in same ch as previous tr, then in last ch, 1 picot, turn.

Special abbreviations

1 picot = ch 3, insert hook downward through 3 front loops at top of group just worked and work 1 slip stitch.

ROW 2: ch 3, skip [1 group, 1 picot, 1 ch], 1 tr in next ch (the center ch of 3), *ch 3, tr2tog, inserting hook first in same ch as previous tr, then in 2nd of next 3-ch, 1 picot; repeat from *, ending tr2tog inserting hook first in same ch as last tr, then in top of last tr, 1 picot, turn.
Repeat row 2.
Fasten off yarn.

⊚ **FOUNDATION CHAIN:** multiple
of 18 chains plus 8.
Make the required length
of foundation chain.

ROW 1: 1 dc into 8th ch from
hook, *ch 2, skip next 2 ch,
1 dc into next ch; rep from *
to end, turn.

ROW 2: ch 5 (counts as 1 dc, ch
2), skip first dc, 1 dc into next
dc, *ch 4, 1 tr into each of next
4 dc, ch 4, 1 dc into next dc, ch
2, 1 dc into next dc; rep from *
to end, working last dc into
3rd of beg skipped 7-ch, turn.

ROW 3: ch 5, skip first dc, 1 dc
into next dc, *ch 4, 1 sc into
each of next 4 tr, ch 4, 1 dc into
next dc, ch 2, 1 dc into next dc;
rep from * to end, working last
dc into 3rd of 5-ch, turn.

ROWS 4 & 5: ch 5, skip first dc,
1 dc into next dc, *ch 4, 1 sc into
each of next 4 sc, ch 4, 1 dc into
next dc, ch 2, 1 dc into next dc;
rep from * to end, working last
dc into 3rd of 5-ch, turn.

Fancy openwork

ROW 6: ch 5, skip first dc, 1 dc
into next dc, *ch 2, [1 tr into next
sc, ch 2] four times, 1 dc into next
dc, ch 2, 1 dc into next dc; rep
from * to end, working last dc
into 3rd of 5-ch, turn.

ROW 7: ch 5, skip first dc, 1 dc
into next dc, *ch 2, [1 dc into
next tr, ch 2] four times, 1 dc into
next dc, ch 2, 1 dc into next dc;
rep from * to end, working last
dc into 3rd of 5-ch, turn.

ROW 8: ch 5, skip first dc, 1 dc
into next dc, *ch 4, 1 tr into each
of next 4 dc, ch 4, 1 dc into next
dc, ch 2, 1 dc into next dc; rep
from * to end, working last dc
into 3rd of 5-ch, turn.

Rep rows 3–8 for length required.
Fasten off yarn.

ch = chain,
see page 18.

dc = double
crochet, see
page 24.

tr = treble
crochet, see
page 26.

Abbreviations
and symbols,
see page 180.

Note

Either side can be
used as RS

Lavender lace

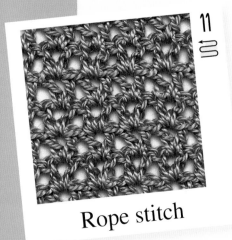

Rope stitch

ch = chain,
see page 18.

sc = single
crochet, see
page 20.

dc = double
crochet, see
page 24.

Abbreviations
and symbols,
see page 180.

🌀 **FOUNDATION CHAIN:** multiple of
3 chains plus 3.
Make the required length
of foundation chain.
ROW 1: 1 dc in 4th ch from hook,
ch 1, 1 dc in next ch, *skip 1 ch,
1 dc in next ch, ch 1, 1 dc in next
ch; repeat from * to last ch, 1 dc
in last ch, turn.
ROW 2: ch 3, skip first 2 dc,
*[1 dc, ch , 1 dc] in 1-ch-sp, skip
2 dc; repeat from *, ending skip
last dc, 1 dc in 3rd of 3-ch, turn.
Repeat row 2.
Fasten off yarn.

🌀 **FOUNDATION CHAIN:** multiple of
10 chains plus 4.
Make the required length of
foundation chain.
ROW 1: 1 dc into 4th ch from
hook, *ch 3, skip next 4 ch,
[1 sc, ch 3, 3 dc] into next ch, skip
next 4 ch, [1 dc, ch 1, 1 dc] into
next ch; rep from * ending last
rep with 2 dc into last ch, turn.
ROW 2: ch 3 (counts as 1 dc), 1 dc
into first dc, *ch 3, 1 sc into 3rd
of next 3-ch, ch 3, 3 dc into sp,
[1 dc, ch 1, 1 dc] into next
1-ch-sp; rep from * ending last
rep with 2 dc into sp made by beg
skipped 3-ch, turn.
ROW 3: ch 3, 1 dc into first dc,
*ch 3, 1 sc into 3rd of next 3-ch,
ch 3, 3 dc into 3-ch-sp, [1 dc, ch
1, 1 dc] into next 1-ch-sp; rep
from * ending last rep with 2 dc
into sp made by 3-ch, turn.
Rep row 3 for length required.
Fasten off yarn.

Mophead stitch

FOUNDATION

CHAIN: multiple of 10 chains plus 2. Make the required length of foundation chain.

ROW 1: 1 sc in 3rd ch from hook, *ch 3, skip 2 ch, 1 sc in each of next 3 ch; repeat from *, ending 1 sc in each of last 2 ch, turn.

ROW 2: ch 1, skip first sc, 1 sc in next sc, 1 sc in 3-ch-sp, *ch 3, skip 1 sc, 1 dc in next sc (the center sc of 3), ch 3, skip 1 sc, 1 sc in 3-ch-sp, 1 sc in each of next 3 sc, 1 sc in 3-ch-sp; repeat from *, ending 1 sc in last 3-ch-sp, 1 sc in last sc, 1 sc in 1-ch, turn.

ROW 3: ch 1, skip first sc, 1 sc in next sc, *ch 3, skip 1 sc, 1 sc in 3-ch-sp, 1 sc in dc, 1 sc in 3-ch-sp, ch 3, skip 1 sc, 1 sc in each of next 3 sc (the center 3 of 5); repeat from *, ending 1 sc in last sc, 1 sc in 1-ch, turn.

ROW 4: ch 6, skip first 2 sc, *1 sc in 3-ch-sp, 1 sc in each of 3 sc, 1 sc in 3-ch-sp, ch 3, skip 1 sc, 1 dc in next sc (the center sc of 3), ch 3, skip 1 sc; repeat from *, ending 1 dc in 1-ch, turn.

ROW 5: ch 1, skip first dc, *1 sc in 3-ch-sp, ch 3, skip 1 sc, 1 sc in each of next 3 sc, (the center 3 of 5), ch 3, skip 1 sc, 1 sc in 3-ch-sp, 1 sc in dc; repeat from *, ending 1 sc under 6 ch, 1 sc in 3rd of these 6-ch, turn.

Repeat rows 2–5.
Fasten off yarn.

ch = chain, see page 18.

sc = single crochet, see page 20.

dc = double crochet, see page 24.

Abbreviations and symbols, see page 180.

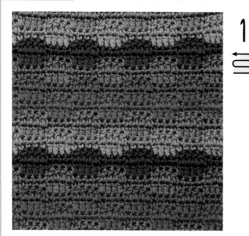

Interlocking colors

Note

Worked in 6 colors, A, B, C, D, E, and F.

ch = chain, see page 18.

sc = single crochet, see page 20.

dc = double crochet, see page 24.

Abbreviations and symbols, see page 180.

◉ **FOUNDATION CHAIN:** Using yarn A, work a multiple of 8 chains plus 5.

ROW 1 (RS): 1 sc into 2nd ch from hook, 1 sc into each of next 3 chs, *1 dc into each of next 4 chs, 1 sc into each of next 4 chs; rep from * to end, turn.

ROW 2: ch 1, 1 sc into each of next 4 sc, *1 dc into each of next 4 dc, 1 sc into each of next 4 sc; rep from * to end, turn.

ROW 3: ch 3 (counts as 1 dc), sk first sc, 1 dc into each of next 3 sc, *1 sc into each of next 4 dc, 1 dc into each of next 4 sc; rep from * to end, turn.

ROW 4: ch 3, sk first st, 1 dc into each of next 3 dc, *1 sc into each of next 4 sc, 1 dc into each of next 4 dc; rep from * to end, working last dc into 3rd of 3-ch, turn.

ROW 5: ch 1, 1 sc into each of next 4 dc, *1 dc into each of next 4 sc, 1 sc into each of next 4 dc; rep from * to end, working last sc into 3rd of 3-ch, turn.

Rep rows 2–5, changing yarns in the following color sequence:

2 rows in yarn A,
2 rows in yarn B,
2 rows in yarn C,
2 rows in yarn D,
2 rows in yarn E,
2 rows in yarn F.

Repeat for length required.

Fasten off yarn.

FOUNDATION CHAIN: multiple of 17 chains plus 3.

Using yarn A, make the required length of foundation chain.

ROW 1 (RS): 1 sc into 2nd ch from hook, 1 sc into each ch, turn.

ROW 2: ch 3, skip first 3 sc, [3 dc into next sc, skip next 2 sc] twice, [3 dc, ch 3, 3 dc] into next sc, * skip next 2 sc, 3 dc into next sc, skip next 2 sc, cl into next sc, skip next 4 sc, cl into next sc, [skip next 2 sc, 3 dc into next sc] once, skip next 2 sc, [3 dc, ch 3, 3 dc] into next sc; rep from * to last 8 sc, skip next 2 sc, [3 dc into next sc, skip next 2 sc] twice, 1 dc into last sc, turn.

ROW 3: ch 3, skip sp between turning ch and next 3-dc group, 3 dc into each of next 3 sps, [3 dc, ch 3, 3 dc] into next 3-ch-sp, * 3 dc into next sp, cl into next sp, skip sp between cls, cl into next sp, 3 dc into next sp, [3 dc, ch 3, 3 dc] into next 3-ch-sp; rep from * to last 3 sps, 3 dc into each of next 2 sps, 1 dc into sp between last 3-dc group and turning ch, turn.

Rep row 3, changing yarns in the following color sequence:
2 rows in yarn A,
2 rows in yarn B,
2 rows in yarn C.
Repeat for length required.
Fasten off yarn.

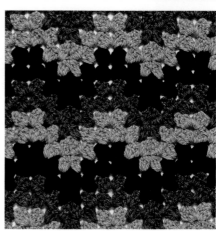

Storm clouds

Special abbreviations

cl = cluster (keeping last loop of each dc on hook, work 3 dc into next stitch or space, yo and draw through all 4 loops on hook).
cls = clusters.

Note

Worked in 3 colors, A, B, and C.

ch = chain, see page 18.

sc = single crochet, see page 20.

dc = double crochet, see page 24.

cl = cluster, see page 46.

Abbreviations and symbols, see page 180.

Cable stitch

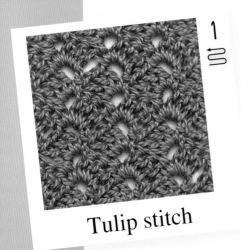

Tulip stitch

ch = chain,
see page 18.

sc = single
crochet, see
page 20.

dc = double
crochet, see
page 24.

Abbreviations
and symbols,
see page 180.

◉ FOUNDATION CHAIN: multiple of 4 chains plus 5.
Make the required length of foundation chain.
ROW 1: 3 dc in 5th ch from hook, skip 3 ch, 1 sc in next ch, *ch 3, 3 dc in same ch as last sc, skip 3 ch, 1 sc in next ch; repeat from *, ending 1 sc in last ch, turn.
ROW 2: ch 4, 3 dc in first of these 4 ch, skip [1 sc, 3 dc], 1 sc in 3-ch-sp, *ch 3, 3 dc in same ch-sp as last sc, skip [1 sc, 3 dc], 1 sc in next 3-ch-sp; repeat from *, working last sc under 4-ch, turn.
Repeat row 2.
Fasten off yarn.

Special abbreviations

1 cable st = Work 1 dc, inserting hook 4 sts to the right in last sc skipped.

◉ FOUNDATION CHAIN: multiple of 4 chains plus 2.
Make the required length of foundation chain.
ROW 1 (WS): 1 sc in 2nd ch from hook, 1 sc in each ch to end, turn.
ROW 2: ch 3, skip first sc, *skip next sc, 1 dc in each of next 3 sc, 1 cable st; repeat from *, ending 1 dc in 1 ch, turn.
ROW 3: ch 1, skip first dc, 1 sc in each dc, ending 1 sc in 3rd of 3-ch, turn.
Repeat rows 2 and 3.
The cables should form vertical rows.
Fasten off yarn.

Bars and diamonds

@ **FOUNDATION CHAIN:** multiple of 8 chains plus 3.
Make the required length of foundation chain.

FOUNDATION ROW (WS): 1 sc into 2nd ch from hook, 1 sc into each ch, turn.

ROW 1: ch 3 (counts as 1 dc), 1 dc into next sc, *skip 2 sc, 1 dc into next sc, ch 3, work block of 3 evenly spaced dc into side of dc just made, skip 2 sc, 1 dc into each of next 3 sc; rep from * ending last rep with 2 dc, turn.

ROW 2: ch 3 (counts as 1 dc), 1 dc into next dc, *ch 2, 1 sc into 3rd of ch 3 at top corner of next block, ch 2, 1 dc into each of next 3 dc; rep from * ending last rep with 2 dc, turn.

ROW 3: ch 3 (counts as 1 dc), 1 dc into next dc, *1 dc into next sc, ch 3, work block of 3 evenly spaced dc into side of dc just made, 1 dc into each of next 3 dc; rep from * ending last rep with 2 dc, turn.

Rep rows 2–3, ending with row 2.

NEXT ROW: ch 1, 1 sc into each of next 2 dc, *2 sc into next 2-ch-sp, 1 sc into next sc, 2 sc into next 2-ch-sp, 1 sc into each of next 3 dc; rep from * ending last rep with 2 sc.
Fasten off yarn.

ch = chain, see page 18.

sc = single crochet, see page 20.

dc = double crochet, see page 24.

Abbreviations and symbols, see page 180.

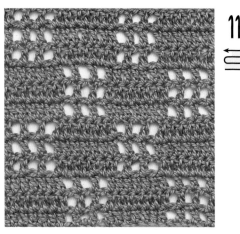

Filet squares

ch = chain,
see page 18.

dc = double
crochet, see
page 24.

Abbreviations
and symbols,
see page 180.

 FOUNDATION CHAIN: multiple of 12 chains plus 3.
Make the required length of foundation chain.

ROW 1: 1 dc in 4th ch from hook, 1 dc in each of next 5 ch, [ch 1, skip 1 ch, 1 dc in next ch] 3 times, *1 dc in each of next 6 ch, [ch 1, skip 1 ch, 1 dc in next ch] 3 times; repeat from * to end, turn.

ROW 2: ch 4, skip [first dc, 1 ch], 1 dc in next dc, [ch 1, skip 1 ch, 1 dc in next dc] twice, 1 dc in each of next 6 dc, *[ch 1, skip 1 ch, 1 dc in next dc] 3 times, 1 dc in each of next 6 dc; repeat from * ending 1 dc in 3rd of 3-ch, turn.

ROW 3: ch 3, skip first dc, *1 dc in each of next 6 dc, [ch 1, skip 1 ch, 1 dc in next dc] 3 times; repeat from *, working last dc in 3rd of 4-ch, turn.

ROW 4: ch 3, skip first dc, *[1 dc in 1-ch-sp, 1 dc in dc] 3 times, [ch 1, skip 1 dc, 1 dc in next dc] 3 times; repeat from *, working last dc in 3rd of 3-ch, turn.

ROW 5: as row 2.
ROW 6: as row 3.
ROW 7: as row 4.
Repeat rows 2–7.
Fasten off yarn.

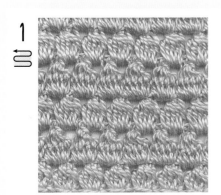

Large clusters

Special abbreviations

cl (cluster) = [yrh, insert hook as given, yrh, pull loop through, yrh, pull through 2 loops] 5 times in same place, yrh, pull through first 5 loops on hook, yrh, pull through both loops on hook.

FOUNDATION CHAIN: multiple of 2 chains plus 2.
Make the required length of foundation chain.
ROW 1: 1 cl in 4th ch from hook, *ch 1, skip 1 ch, 1 cl in next ch; repeat from * to end, turn.
ROW 2: ch 3, skip first cl, *1 cl in next ch-sp, ch 1, skip next cl; repeat from *, ending 1 cl under 3-ch, turn.
Repeat row 2.
Fasten off yarn.

Tiny textures

FOUNDATION CHAIN: multiple of 2 chains plus 1.
Make the required length of foundation chain.
FOUNDATION ROW (RS): work 1 sc into 2nd ch from hook, 1 sc into each chain to end, turn.
ROW 1: ch 1, 1 sc in first sc, *ch 1, skip 1 sc, 1 sc into next sc; rep from * to end, turn.
ROW 2: ch 1, 1 sc in first sc, *1 dc in next ch 1 sp, 1 sc into next sc; rep from * to end, turn.
ROW 3: ch 1, 1 sc in first sc, *ch 1, skip 1 sc, 1 sc into next sc; rep from * to end, turn.
Rep rows 2–3, ending with a 3rd row.
NEXT ROW: work 1 sc in each st along row.
Fasten off yarn.

ch = chain, see page 18.

sc = single crochet, see page 20.

dc = double crochet, see page 24.

cl = cluster, see page 46.

Abbreviations and symbols, see page 180.

111

Relief doubles

ch = chain,
see page 18.

sc = single
crochet, see
page 20.

dc = double
crochet, see
page 24.

Abbreviations
and symbols,
see page 180.

Special abbreviations

frdc (front raised double) =
yo, insert the hook from the
front and from right to left
around the stem of the stitch,
and complete the stitch.

🌀 **FOUNDATION CHAIN:** multiple
of 2 chains plus 1.
Make the required length of
foundation chain.
ROW 1: 1 dc in 4th ch from hook,
1 dc in each ch to end, turn.
ROW 2: ch 1, skip first dc, 1 sc in
each dc, ending 1 sc in 3rd of
3-ch, turn.

ROW 3: ch 2, skip first sc, *1 frdc
around dc below next sc, skip this
sc, 1 sc in next sc; repeat from *,
ending 1 sc in 1-ch, turn.
ROW 4: ch 1, skip first sc, *1 sc in
frdc, 1 sc in sc; repeat from *,
ending 1 sc in last frdc, 1 sc in
2nd of 2-ch, turn.
ROW 5: ch 2, skip first sc, *1 frdc
around frdc below next sc, skip
this sc, 1 sc in next sc; repeat from
*, ending 1 sc in 1-ch, turn.
Repeat rows 4–5.
Fasten off yarn.

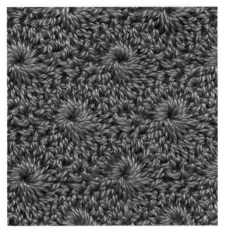

Star burst stitch

🌀 **FOUNDATION CHAIN:** multiple of 8 chains plus 1.
Make the required length of foundation chain.

ROW 1 (WS): skip 4 ch, *9 dc in next ch, skip 3 ch, 1 sc in next ch, skip 3 ch; repeat from *, ending 1 sc in last ch, turn.

ROW 2: ch 3, skip first sc, dc4tog over next 4 dc, *ch 4, 1 sc in next dc (the center dc of 9), ch 3, dc9tog over [next 4 dc, 1 sc, 4 dc]; repeat from *, ending dc5tog over [last 4 dc and 1 ch].

ROW 3: ch 4, 4 dc in top of dc5tog, *skip 3 ch, 1 sc in sc, skip 4 ch, 9 dc in top of dc9tog; repeat from *, ending 5 dc in top of dc4tog, turn.

ROW 4: ch 4, skip first dc, *dc9tog over [next 4 dc, 1 sc, 4 dc], ch 4, 1 sc in next dc (the center dc of 9), ch 3; repeat from *, ending 1 sc in 4th of 4-ch, turn.

ROW 5: ch 1, skip first sc, *skip 4 ch, 9 dc in top of dc9tog, skip 3 ch, 1 sc in sc; repeat from *, working last sc in first of 4-ch, turn.
Repeat rows 2–5.
Fasten off yarn.

ch = chain, see page 18.

sc = single crochet, see page 20.

dc = double crochet, see page 24.

dc4tog = double crochet 4 sts tog, see page 39.

dc5tog = double crochet 5 sts tog, see page 39.

dc9tog = double crochet 9 sts tog, see page 39.

Abbreviations and symbols, see page 180.

Regatta

Note

Worked in 5 colors, A, B, C, D, and E.

ROW 3: ch 3, 2 dc into first sc, * skip next 3 dc, 1 sc into first of 3 ch, ch 3, 1 dc into each of next 2 ch, 1 dc into next sc; rep from * ending last rep with skip next 2 dc, 1 sc into 3rd of 3-ch, turn.

Rep row 3, changing yarns in the following color sequence:

2 rows in yarn A,
2 rows in yarn B,
2 rows in yarn C,
2 rows in yarn D,
2 rows in yarn E.
Repeat for length required.
Fasten off yarn.

ch = chain, see page 18.

sc = single crochet, see page 20.

dc = double crochet, see page 24.

Abbreviations and symbols, see page 180.

FOUNDATION CHAIN: multiple of 7 chains plus 2.
Using yarn A, make the required length of foundation chain.
ROW 1 (RS): 1 dc into 4th ch from hook, 2 dc into next ch, * skip next 3 ch, 1 sc into next ch, ch 3, 1 dc into each of next 3 ch; rep from * to last 4 ch, skip next 3 ch, 1 sc into last ch, turn.
ROW 2: ch 3, 2 dc into first sc, * skip next 3 dc, 1 sc into first of 3 ch, ch 3, 1 dc into each of next 2 ch, 1 dc into next sc; rep from * ending last rep with skip next 3 dc, 1 sc into 3rd of beg 3-ch, turn.

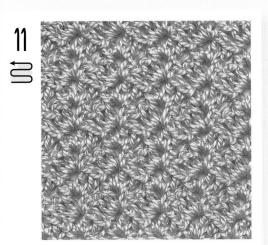

Open scallop

ch = chain,
see page 18.

dc = double
crochet, see
page 24.

Abbreviations
and symbols,
see page 180.

FOUNDATION CHAIN: multiple of 6 chains plus 3.

Make the required length of foundation chain.

ROW 1: [2 dc, ch 1, 2 dc] in 4th ch from hook, *1 grp, [2 dc, ch 1, 2 dc] in next ch; repeat from * to last 3 ch, 1 grp ending in last ch, turn.

ROW 2: ch 3, skip [first grp, 1 dc], 1 dc in next dc, *[2 dc, ch 1, 2 dc] in 1-ch-sp, 1 grp; repeat from *, ending last grp in 3rd of 3-ch, turn.

Repeat row 2.

Special abbreviations

grp (group) = 2 linked doubles, worked as follows: *yrh, insert hook in next st, yrh, pull loop through, yrh, pull through first 2 loops*, skip next 3 sts; repeat * to * in next st, yrh, pull through first 2 loops, yrh, pull through both loops on hook.

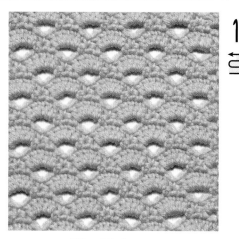

Shell lace

ch = chain,
see page 18.

sc = single
crochet, see
page 20.

dc = double
crochet, see
page 24.

Abbreviations
and symbols,
see page 180.

FOUNDATION CHAIN: multiple of 9 chains plus 5.
Make the required length of foundation chain.

FOUNDATION ROW (WS): 1 sc into 2nd ch from hook, 1 sc into next ch, *ch 3, skip 3 ch, 1 sc into each of next 3 ch; rep from * to last 5 ch, ch 3, skip 3 ch, 1 sc into each of last 2 ch, turn.

ROW 1 (RS): ch 1, 1 sc into first sc, * 5 dc into 3-ch-sp, skip 1 sc, 1 sc into next sc; rep from * to end, turn.

ROW 2: ch 3, *1 sc into 2nd, 3rd, and 4th stitches of 5-dc-group, ch 3; rep from * to end, ending with 1 sc into 2nd, 3rd and 4th stitches of 5 dc group, ch 2, 1 sc into last st, turn.

ROW 3: ch 3, 2 dc into 2-ch-sp, skip 1 sc, 1 sc into next sc, *5 dc into 3-ch-sp, skip 1 sc, 1 sc into next sc; rep from * to end, 3 dc into last 3-ch-sp, turn.

ROW 4: ch 1, 1 sc into each of first 2 dc, *ch 3, 1 sc into 2nd, 3rd and 4th stitches of 5-dc-group; rep from * to end, ending with ch 3, 1 sc into 2nd dc, 1 sc into 3rd of 3-ch, turn.

Rep rows 1–4 four times, ending with a 4th row.
Fasten off yarn.

Special abbreviations

dc2tog = work 2 double crochet stitches together to decrease 1 stitch (work 2 incomplete double crochet stitches, keeping last loop of each stitch on the hook. Yarn over hook and draw through all 3 loops on hook).

FOUNDATION CHAIN: multiple of 12 chains plus 3.
Using yarn A, make the required length of foundation chain.

ROW 1 (RS): 1 dc into 4th ch from hook, * 1 dc into each of next 3 ch, [dc2tog] twice, 1 dc into each of next 3 ch, [2 dc into next ch] twice; rep from * ending last rep with 2 dc into last ch, turn.

ROW 2: ch 3, 1 dc into same st, * 1 dc into each of next 3 dc, [dc2tog] twice, 1 dc into each of next 3 dc, [2 dc into next dc] twice; rep from * ending last rep with 2 dc into 3rd of beg skipped 3-ch, turn.

ROW 3: ch 3, 1 dc into same st, * 1 dc into each of next 3 dc, [dc2tog] twice, 1 dc into each of next 3 dc, [2 dc into next dc] twice; rep from * ending last rep with 2 dc into 3rd of 3-ch, turn.

Soft waves

Note

Worked in 5 colors, A, B, C, D, and E.

Rep row 3, changing yarns in the following color sequence:
4 rows in yarn A,
1 row in yarn B,
2 rows in yarn C,
3 rows in yarn D,
4 rows in yarn E.
Repeat for length required.
Fasten off yarn.

ch = chain, see page 18.

dc = double crochet, see page 24.

dc2tog = double crochet 2 sts tog, see page 39.

Abbreviations and symbols, see page 180.

Sultan stitch

ch = chain,
see page 18.

sc = single
crochet, see
page 20.

dc = double
crochet, see
page 24.

Abbreviations
and symbols,
see page 180.

🌀 **FOUNDATION CHAIN:** multiple of 4 chains plus 5.

Make the required length of foundation chain.

ROW 1: [1 dc, ch 2, 1 dc] in 6th ch from hook, *skip 3 ch, [1 dc, ch 2, 1 dc] in next ch; repeat from * to last 3 ch, skip 2 ch, 1 dc in last ch, turn.

ROW 2: ch 3, skip first 2 dc, *4 dc in 2-ch-sp, skip 2 dc; repeat from *, ending skip last dc, 1 dc in next ch, turn.

ROW 3: ch 4, 1 dc in sp between first 2 dc, *skip group of 4 dc, [1 dc, ch 2, 1 dc] in sp before next group; repeat from *, ending [1 dc, ch 1, 1 dc] in sp before 3-ch, turn.

ROW 4: ch 3, skip first dc, 2 dc in 1-ch-sp, *skip 2 dc, 4 dc in 2-ch-sp; repeat from *, ending 3 dc under 4-ch, turn.

ROW 5: ch 3, skip first 3 dc, *[1 dc, ch 2, 1 dc] in sp before next group, skip group of 4-dc; repeat from *, ending skip last 2 dc, 1 dc in sp before 3-ch, turn.

Repeat rows 2–5.

Fasten off yarn.

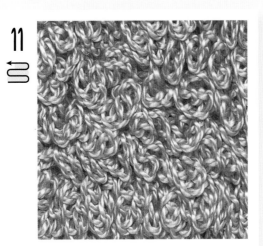

Chain loop stitch

🌀 **FOUNDATION CHAIN:** multiple of any number plus 2.

Make the required length of foundation chain loosely.

ROW 1 (WS): 1 exsc in 3rd ch from hook, 1 exsc in each ch to end, turn.

ROW 2: ch 1, 1 sc in front loop of first exsc, *6 ch, 1 sc in front loop of next exsc; repeat from *, ending 1 sc in front loop of last exsc, turn.

ROW 3: ch 1, 1 exsc in empty loop of first exsc 2 rows below, 1 exsc in empty loop of each exsc 2 rows below to end, turn.

Repeat rows 2–3.

Special abbreviations

exsc (extended single crochet) = insert the hook into the stitch or ch indicated, yo, draw the yarn through, yo and draw the yarn through the loop only, yo and draw the yarn through both loops on the hook.

ch = chain, see page 18.

sc = single crochet, see page 20.

Abbreviations and symbols, see page 180.

Waterbeach

ch = chain,
see page 18.

sc = single
crochet, see
page 20.

dc = double
crochet, see
page 24.

dc2tog =
double crochet
2 sts tog, see
page 39.

hdc3tog = half
double crochet
3 sts tog, see
page 39.

Abbreviations
and symbols,
see page 180.

Note

Worked in 3 colors, A, B, and C.

🌀 **FOUNDATION CHAIN:** multiple of 17 chains plus 2.
Using yarn A, make the required length of foundation chain.

ROW 1 (RS): 1 dc into 4th ch from hook, [dc2tog over next 2 ch] twice, * [ch 1, hdc3tog into next ch] five times, 1 ch, ** [dc2tog over next 2 ch] six times; rep from * ending last rep at ** when 6 ch rem, [dc2tog over next 2 ch] three times, turn.

ROW 2: ch 1, 1 sc into first st and into each st and 1-ch-sp to end of row excluding beg skipped 3-ch, turn.

ROW 3: ch 3, skip first st, 1 dc into next st, [dc2tog over next 2 sts] twice, * [ch 1, hdc3tog into next st] five times, 1 ch, ** [dc2tog over next 2 sts] six times; rep from * ending last rep at ** when 6 sts rem, [dc2tog over next 2 sts] three times, skip 3-ch, turn.

Rep rows 2 and 3, changing yarns in the foll color sequence:
4 rows in yarn A,
2 rows in yarn B,
2 rows in yarn C.
Repeat for length required.
Fasten off yarn.

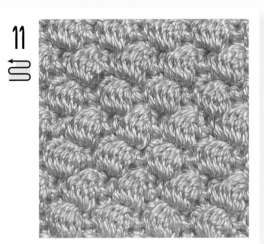

Honeycomb stitch

🌀 **FOUNDATION CHAIN:** multiple of 3 chains plus 1.

Make the required length of foundation chain.

ROW 1: 1 sc in 2nd ch from hook, 1 sc in each ch to end, turn.

ROW 2: ch 1, 1 sc in each of first 2 sc, *1 cl in next sc, 1 sc in each of next 2 sc; repeat from *, ending 1 cl in last sc, turn.

ROW 3: ch 1, *1 sc in cl, 1 sc in each of next 2 sc; repeat from * to end, turn.

ROW 4: ch 1, 1 cl in first sc, *1 sc in each of next 2 sc, 1 cl in next sc; repeat from *, ending 1 sc in each of last 2 sc, turn.

Special abbreviations

cl (cluster) = 5 doubles together, all worked into same stitch.

ROW 5: ch 1, 1 sc in first sc, 1 sc in next sc, *1 sc in cl, 1 sc in each of next 2 sc; repeat from *, ending 1 sc in last cl, turn.

Repeat rows 2–5.

ch = chain, see page 18.

sc = single crochet, see page 20.

dc = double crochet, see page 24.

cl = cluster, see page 46.

Abbreviations and symbols, see page 180.

Bamboo stitch

ch = chain,
see page 18.

sl st = slip stitch,
see page 19.

dc = double
crochet, see
page 24.

Abbreviations
and symbols,
see page 180.

🌀 **FOUNDATION CHAIN:** multiple of 4 chains plus 4.

Using A, make the required length of foundation chain.

ROW 1: using A, 1 dc in 4th ch from hook, *ch 2, skip 2 ch, 1 dc in each of next 2 ch; repeat from * to end, slip loop from hook onto holder, do not turn. Return to beginning of row, join B to 3rd of 3-ch, ch 2, skip next dc, * 1 dc in each of 2 empty foundation ch below, (enclosing 2 ch in A), ch 2, skip 2 dc in A; repeat from *, ending ch 2, skip 1 dc in A, pull loop of A from holder through loop on hook, turn. Remove holder.

Note

Worked in 2 colors, A and B. A stitch holder is required.

ROW 2: using A, ch 3, skip first dc in A below, 1 dc in next dc in A below (enclosing 1 ch in B), *ch 2, skip 2 dc in B, 1 dc in each of 2 dc in A below (enclosing 2 ch in B); repeat from *, ending 1 dc in 3rd of 3 ch in A below, slip loop from hook onto holder, do not turn. Return to beginning of row, using B, 1 sl st in 3rd of 3-ch in A, ch 2, skip next dc, *1 dc in each of 2 dc in B below (enclosing 2 ch in A), ch 2, skip 2 dc in A; repeat from *, ending ch 2, skip 1 dc in A, pull loop of A from holder through loop on hook, turn. Remove holder.

Repeat row 2.

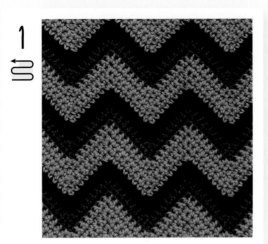

Chocolate delight

FOUNDATION CHAIN: multiple of 16 chains plus 2.

Using yarn A, make the required length of foundation chain.

ROW 1 (RS): 2 sc into 2nd ch from hook, * 1 sc into each of next 7 ch, skip next ch, 1 sc into each of next 7 ch, 3 sc into next ch; rep from * to end, ending last rep with 2 sc into last ch, turn.

ROW 2: ch 1, 2 sc into first sc, * 1 sc into each of next 7 sc, skip next 2 sc, 1 sc into each of next 7 sc, 3 sc into next sc; rep from * to end, ending last rep with 2 sc into last sc, turn.

Note

Worked in 3 colors, A, B, and C.

Rep row 2, changing yarns in the following color sequence:
4 rows in yarn A,
2 rows in yarn B,
2 rows in yarn C.
Repeat for length required.
Fasten off yarn.

ch = chain, see page 18.

sc = single crochet, see page 20.

Abbreviations and symbols, see page 180.

11

Rake stitch

ch = chain,
see page 18.

sc = single
crochet, see
page 20.

Abbreviations
and symbols,
see page 180.

Notes

Worked in 2 colors, A and B.

⊚ **FOUNDATION CHAIN:** multiple of 10 chains plus 7.
Using A, make the required length of foundation chain.
ROW 1 (WS): using A, 1 sc in 2nd ch from hook, 1 sc in each ch, changing to B at end, turn.
Do not cut A.
ROW 2: using B, ch 1, 1 sc in each st ending 1 sc in 1-ch, turn.
ROW 3: As row 2, changing to A at end. Do not cut B.

ROW 4: using A, ch 1, *[1 sc into sc in A, 2 rows below next sc] 5 times, 1 sc in each of next 5 sc; repeat from * ending [1 sc into sc in A, 2 rows below next sc] 5 times, 1 sc in 1 ch, turn.
ROW 5: using A, ch 1, 1 sc in each st ending 1 sc in 1-ch, turn, changing to B at end.
Do not cut A.
ROW 6: using B, ch 1, *1 sc in each of next 5 sc, [1 sc into sc in B, 2 rows below next sc] 5 times; repeat from * ending 1 sc in each of last 5 sc, 1 sc in 1-ch, turn.
Repeat rows 3–6.

⊚ FOUNDATION CHAIN: multiple of 8 chains plus 4.

Make the required length of foundation chain.

FOUNDATION ROW: 1 dc into 4th ch from hook, 1 dc into each ch to end, turn.

ROW 1: ch 2, skip first dc, * frdc round each of next 4 dc, brdc round each of next 4 dc; rep from * ending last rep with 1 dc into 3rd of beg skipped 3-ch, turn.

ROWS 2, 3, 4: ch 2, skip first dc, * frdc round each of next 4 dc, brdc round each of next 4 dc; rep from * ending last rep with 1 dc into 2nd of 2-ch, turn.

ROWS 5, 6, 7, 8: ch 2, skip first dc, * brdc round each of next 4 dc, frdc round each of next 4 dc; rep from * ending last rep with 1 dc into 2nd of 2-ch, turn.

ROW 9: ch 2, skip first dc, * frdc round each of next 4 dc, brdc round each of next 4 dc; rep from * ending last rep with 1 dc into 2nd of 2-ch, turn.

Rep rows 2–9 for length required, ending with a row 4.

Basketweave

Special abbreviations

frdc (front raised double) = yo, insert the hook from the front and from right to left around the stem of the stitch, and complete the stitch.

brdc (back raised double) = yo, insert the hook from the back and from right to left around the stem of the stitch, and complete the stitch.

ch = chain, see page 18.

dc = double crochet, see page 24.

Abbreviations and symbols, see page 180.

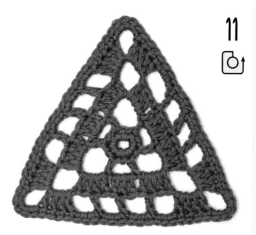

11

Fretwork triangle

ch = chain,
see page 18.

sl st = slip stitch,
see page 19.

sc = single
crochet, see
page 20.

dc = double
crochet, see
page 24.

Abbreviations
and symbols,
see page 180.

FOUNDATION RING: ch 6 and join with sl st to form a ring.

ROUND 1: ch 1, work 12 sc into ring, join with sl st into first sc.

ROUND 2: ch 10 (counts as 1 dc, ch 7), skip first 2 sc, * 1 dc into next sc, ch 3, skip 1 sc, 1 dc into next sc, ch 7, skip 1 sc; rep from * once, 1 dc into next sc, ch 3, skip last sc, join with sl st into 3rd ch of 10-ch. (6 spaced dc).

ROUND 3: ch 3 (counts as 1 dc), [3 dc, ch 7, 4 dc] into next 7-ch-sp, * 3 dc into next 3-ch-sp, [4 dc, ch 7, 4 dc] into next 7-ch-sp; rep from * once, 3 dc into 3-ch-sp, join with sl st into 3rd ch of 3-ch.

ROUND 4: ch 6 (counts as 1 dc, ch 3), * [4 dc, ch 5, 4 dc] into next 7-ch-sp, ch 3, skip 2 dc, 1 dc into next dc, ch 3, skip 2 dc, 1 dc into next dc, ch 3, ** skip 2 dc, 1 dc into next dc, ch 3; rep from * once and from * to ** once, join with sl st into 3rd ch of 6-ch.

ROUND 5: ch 1, work 1 sc in each dc around triangle, working 3 sc into each 3-ch-sp and 5 sc into each 5-ch-sp, join with sl st into first sc.

Fasten off yarn.

Cathedral window

🌀 **FOUNDATION RING:** ch 6 and join with sl st to form a ring.

ROUND 1: ch 3 (counts as 1 dc), work 14 dc into ring, join with sl st into 3rd of 3-ch. (15 dc).

ROUND 2: ch 3 (counts as 1 dc), 1 dc into each of next 4 dc, ch 5, [1 dc into each of next 5 dc, ch 5] twice, join with sl st into 3rd ch of 3-ch.

ROUND 3: ch 3 (counts as 1 dc), 1 dc into each of next 4 dc, [5 dc, ch 3, 5 dc] into 5-ch-sp, * 1 dc into each of next 5 dc, [5 dc, ch 3, 5 dc] into 5-ch-sp; rep from * to end, join with sl st into 3rd ch of 3-ch.

ROUND 4: ch 3 (counts as 1 dc), work 1 dc into each dc around triangle, working [3 dc, ch 1, 3 dc] into each 3-ch-sp, join with sl st into 3rd ch of 3-ch. Fasten off yarn.

ch = chain, see page 18.

sl st = slip stitch, see page 19.

dc = double crochet, see page 24.

Abbreviations and symbols, see page 180.

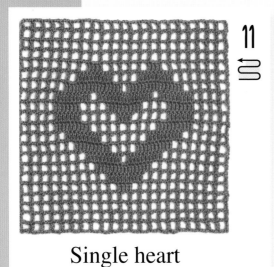

Single heart

ch = chain,
see page 18.

dc = double
crochet, see
page 24.

Abbreviations
and symbols,
see page 180.

Special abbreviations

open mesh = ch 2, 1 dc into
the next dc or foundation ch.
solid mesh = 2 dc into the
2-ch-sp, 1 dc into the next dc.

MOTIF SIZE: 13 blocks high by
13 blocks wide.
Starting at the bottom right-hand
corner of the chart, work the
blocks and spaces from the chart
in filet crochet (see page 78).
When following the chart, read
odd-numbered (RS) rows from
right to left and even-numbered
(WS) rows from left to right.
FOUNDATION CHAIN: ch 44.
ROW 1: 1 dc in 8th ch from hook,
*ch 2, skip 2 ch, 1 dc into the
next ch; rep from * to the end
of the row.
Work 3 rows of open mesh.
Centering the motif, cont working
from chart until completed.
Work 4 rows of open mesh.
Fasten off yarn.

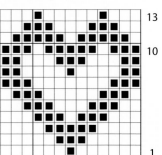

☐   Open mesh

■   Solid mesh

Note

Worked in 3 colors, A, B, and C.

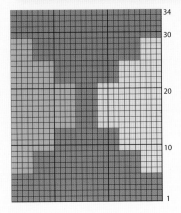

■ A
■ B
□ C

Hourglass

🌀 **FOUNDATION CHAIN:** using yarn A, ch 29.

WORKING THE PATTERN: when following the chart, read odd-numbered rows (right side rows) from right to left and even-numbered rows (wrong side rows) from left to right. Starting at the bottom right-hand corner of the chart, work the 34 row pattern from the chart in sc. On the first row, work first sc into 2nd ch from hook, 1 sc into each ch along row.
(28 sc)
Cont working from chart starting from row 2.
Fasten off yarn.

ch = chain, see page 18.

sc = single crochet, see page 20.

Abbreviations and symbols, see page 180.

Square target

Note

Worked in 3 colors, A, B, and C.

ch = chain, see page 18.

sl st = slip stitch, see page 19.

sc = single crochet, see page 20.

dc = double crochet, see page 24.

Abbreviations and symbols, see page 180.

🌀 **FOUNDATION RING:** using yarn A, ch 4 and join with sl st to form a ring.

ROUND 1: ch 5 (counts as 1 dc, ch 2), [3 dc into ring, ch 2] 3 times, 2 dc into ring, join with sl st into 3rd of 5-ch. (Four grps [page 137] of 3 dc, four 2-ch-spaces forming corners)

ROUND 2: sl st into 2-ch-sp, ch 7 (counts as 1 dc, ch 4), *2 dc into same 2-ch-sp, 1 dc into each dc across side of square, **2 dc into next 2-ch-sp, ch 4; rep from * twice and from * to ** again, 1 dc into last 2-ch-sp, join with sl st to 3rd of 7-ch. (Four grps of 7 dc, four 4ch spaces forming corners) Break off yarn A. Join yarn B to 4-ch-sp.

ROUND 3: ch 7 (counts as 1 dc, ch 4), *2 dc into same 4-ch-sp, 1 dc into each dc across side of square, **2 dc into next 4-ch-sp, ch 4; rep from * twice and from * to ** again, 1 dc into last 4-ch-sp, join with sl st to 3rd of 7-ch. (Four grps of 11 dc, four ch 4 spaces forming corners) Break off yarn B. Join yarn C to 4-ch-sp.

ROUND 4: rep round 3. (Four grps of 15 dc, four 4-ch-spaces forming corners) Break off yarn C. Join yarn B to 4-ch-sp

ROUND 5: rep round 3. (Four grps of 19 dc, four 4-ch-spaces forming corners) Break off yarn B. Join yarn A to 4-ch-sp.

ROUND 6: rep round 3. (Four grps of 23 dc, four 4-ch-spaces forming corners)

ROUND 7: ch 1, 1 sc into each dc in previous round, working [2 sc, ch 1, 2 sc] into each 4-ch-corner-sp, join with sl st into first sc.

ROUND 8: ch 1, 1 sc into each sc in previous round, working ch 2 at each corner, join with sl st into first sc.

Fasten off yarn.

🌀 **FOUNDATION RING:** ch 6 and join with sl st to form a ring.
ROUND 1: ch 3 (counts as 1 dc), 15 dc into ring, join with sl st into 3rd of ch 3.
ROUND 2: ch 3 (counts as 1 dc), 2 dc into same place, ch 2, skip 1 dc, 1 dc into next dc, ch 2, skip 1 dc, *3 dc into next dc, ch 2, skip 1 dc, 1 dc into next dc, ch 2, skip 1 dc; rep from * twice, join with sl st into 3rd of 3-ch.
ROUND 3: ch 3 (counts as 1 dc), 5 dc into next dc, *1 dc into next dc, [ch 2, 1 dc into next dc] twice, 5 dc into next dc; rep from * twice, [1 dc into next dc, ch 2] twice, join with sl st into 3rd of 3-ch.
ROUND 4: ch 3 (counts as 1 dc), 1 dc into each of next 2 dc, 5 dc into next dc, *1 dc into each of next 3 dc, ch 2, 1 dc into next dc, ch 2, 1 dc into each of next 3 dc, 5 dc into next dc; rep from * twice, 1 dc into each of next 3 dc, ch 2, 1 dc into next dc, ch 2, join with sl st into 3rd of 3-ch.
ROUND 5: ch 3 (counts as 1 dc), 1 dc into each of next 4 dc, 5 dc into next dc, *1 dc into each of next 5 dc, ch 2, 1 dc into next dc, ch 2, 1 dc into each of next 5 dc, 5 dc into next dc; rep from * twice, 1 dc into each of next 5 dc, ch 2, 1 dc into next dc, ch 2, join with sl st into 3rd of 3-ch.

Lacy cross

ROUND 6: ch 3 (counts as 1 dc), 1 dc into each of next 6 dc, 5 dc into next dc, *1 dc into each of next 7 dc, ch 2, 1 dc into next dc, ch 2, 1 dc into each of next 7 dc, 5 dc into next dc; rep from * twice, 1 dc into each of next 7 dc, ch 2, 1 dc into next dc, ch 2, join with sl st into 3rd of 3-ch.
ROUND 7: ch 3 (counts as 1 dc), work 1 dc into each dc and 2 dc into each 2-ch-sp of previous round, working [2 dc, ch 1, 2 dc] into center st of each 5 dc corner group, join with sl st into 3rd of 3-ch.
Fasten off yarn.

ch = chain, see page 18.

sl st = slip stitch, see page 19.

dc = double crochet, see page 24.

Abbreviations and symbols, see page 180.

Briar Rose

ch = chain,
see page 18.

sl st = slip stitch,
see page 19.

sc = single
crochet, see
page 20.

hdc = half
double crochet,
see page 22.

dc = double
crochet, see
page 24.

Abbreviations
and symbols,
see page 180.

Note

Worked in 4 colors, A, B, C, and D.

🌀 **FOUNDATION RING:** using yarn A, ch 6 and join with sl st to form a ring.

ROUND 1: ch 1, 16 sc into ring, join with sl st into first sc. (16 sc)

ROUND 2: ch 6 (counts as 1 dc, ch 3), skip 2 sc, [1 dc into next sc, ch 3, skip 1 sc] 7 times; join with sl st into 3rd of 6-ch. (8 spaced dc)

Break off yarn A.

Join yarn B to any 3-ch-sp,

ROUND 3: ch 1 [1 sc, 1 hdc, 1 dc, 1 hdc, 1 sc] into same sp, *[1 sc, 1 hdc, 1 dc, 1 hdc, 1 sc] into next 3-ch-sp; rep from * 6 times, join with sl st into first sc.
(8 petals made)

ROUND 4: ch 1, 1 sc into each sc and hdc of previous round, working 3 sc into each dc, join with sl st into first sc.

Break off yarn B. Join yarn C to 2nd sc of any petal.

ROUND 5: ch 1, 1 sc into same place, *ch 5, skip 3 sc, 1 sc into next sc, ch 7, skip 2 sc, 1 sc into next sc, ch 5, skip 3 sc, 1 sc into next sc, ch 2, skip 2 sc, **1 sc into next sc; rep from * twice and from * to ** once again, join with sl st into first sc.

ROUND 6: ch 2 (counts as 1 hdc), 3 hdc into next 5-ch-sp, * [4 dc, ch 3, 4 dc] into next 7-ch-sp, 4 hdc into next 5-ch-sp, 2 hdc into next 2-ch-sp, **4 hdc into next 5-ch-sp; rep from * twice and from * to ** once again, join with sl st into 2nd of 2-ch.

Break off yarn C. Join yarn D to any 3-ch-corner-sp.

ROUND 7: ch 3 (counts as 1 dc), [1 dc, ch 2, 2 dc] into same sp, *1 dc into each of next 4 dc, 1 dc into each of next 3 hdc, ch 1, skip 1 hdc, 1 dc into each of next 2 hdc, ch 1, skip 1 hdc, 1 dc into each of next 3 hdc, 1 dc into each of next 4 dc, **[2 dc, ch 2, 2 dc] into next 3-ch-corner-sp; rep from * twice and from * to ** once again, join with sl st into 3rd of 3-ch.

ROUND 8: ch 3 (counts as 1 dc), 1 dc into next dc, *[2 dc, ch 2, 2 dc] into next 2-ch-corner-sp, **1 dc into each of next 20 dc; rep from * twice and from * to ** once again, 1 dc into each of next 18 dc, join with sl st into 3rd of 3-ch.

ROUND 9: ch 1, 1 sc into same place, 1 sc into each dc of previous round, working 3 sc into each 2-ch-corner-sp, join with sl st into first sc.

Fasten off yarn.

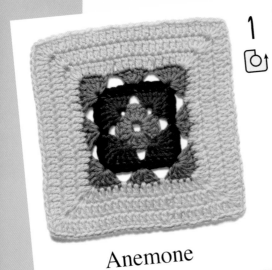

Anemone

Note

Worked in 5 colors, A, B, C, D, and E.

ch = chain, see page 18.

sl st = slip stitch, see page 19.

sc = single crochet, see page 20.

dc = double crochet, see page 24.

Abbreviations and symbols, see page 180.

🌀 **FOUNDATION RING:** using yarn A, ch 4 and join with sl st to form a ring.

ROUND 1: ch 3 (counts as 1 dc), 3 dc into ring, ch 1, *4 dc into ring, ch 1; rep from * twice, join with sl st into 3rd of 3-ch. Break off yarn A. Join yarn B to any 1-ch-sp.

ROUND 2: ch 3 (counts as 1 dc), [3 dc, ch 1, 4 dc] into next 1-ch-sp (corner made), ch 1, *[4 dc, ch 1, 4 dc into next 1-ch-sp, ch 1; rep from * twice, join with sl st into 3rd of 3-ch. (Four corners made) Break off yarn B. Join yarn C.

ROUND 3: ch 1, 1 sc into same place, 1 sc into each dc and 1-ch-sp of previous round, join with sl st into first sc.

Break off yarn C. Join yarn D into any corner sc.

ROUND 4: ch 3 (counts as 1 dc), [3 dc, ch 1, 4 dc] into same sc, ch 1, *skip 4 sc, [2 dc, ch 1, 2 dc] into next sc, ch 1, skip 4 sc, **[4 dc, ch 1, 4 dc] into next sc, ch 1; rep from * twice and from * to ** once again, join with sl st into 3rd of 3-ch. Break off yarn D. Join yarn E to first dc of any corner group.

ROUND 5: ch 3 (counts as 1 dc), work 1 dc into each dc of previous round, working 1 dc into each 1-ch-sp along sides of square and [2 dc, ch 1, 2 dc] into each 1-ch-corner-sp, join with sl st into 3rd of 3-ch.

ROUNDS 6 & 7: ch 3 (counts as 1 dc), work 1 dc into each dc of previous round, working [2 dc, ch 1, 2 dc] into each 1-ch-corner-sp, join with sl st into 3rd of 3-ch. Fasten off yarn.

Special abbreviations

beg cl = beginning cluster made from 5 treble stitches.
cl = cluster made from 6 treble stitches.

Tricolor square

🌀 **FOUNDATION RING:** using yarn A, ch 8 and join with sl st to form a ring.

ROUND 1: ch 4 (counts as 1 tr), 5 tr, [ch 3, 6 tr into ring] 3 times, ch 3, join with sl st into 4th of 4-ch.

ROUND 2: ch 4 (counts as 1 tr), beg cl into each of next 5 tr, *ch 5, sl st into 2nd of ch-3, ch 5, **cl into next 6 tr; rep from * twice and from * to ** once again, join with sl st into 4th of 4-ch. Break off yarn A. Join yarn B to top of any cl.

ROUND 3: *[3 tr, ch 1, 3 tr, ch 2, 3 tr, ch 1, 3 tr] into next 3-ch-sp of round 1, sl st into top of next cl; rep from * 3 times, join with sl st into top of first cl. Break off yarn B. Join yarn A to sl st at top of any cl.

ROUND 4: ch 4 (counts as 1tr) 5 tr into same place, *[6 tr, ch 2, 6 tr] into next 2-ch-sp, **6 tr into sl st at top of next cl; rep from * twice, and from * to ** once again, join with sl st into 4th of 4-ch. Break off yarn A. Join yarn C to last sl st of previous round.

ROUND 5: ch 1, 1 sc into each of

Note

Worked in 3 colors, A, B, and C.

next 6 tr, 1 dc into 1-ch-sp between groups of tr worked on round 3, *1 sc into each of next 6 tr, 3 sc into 2-ch-corner-sp, **[1 sc into each of next 6 tr, 1 dc into 1-ch-sp between groups of tr worked on round 3] twice; rep from * twice and from * to ** once again, 1 sc into each of next 6 tr, 1 dc into 1-ch-sp between groups of tr worked on round 3, join with sl st into first sc.

ROUND 6: ch 3 (counts as 1 dc), 1 dc into each sc and dc of previous round, working 3 dc into center st of each 3 sc corner group, join with sl st into 3rd of 3-ch. Fasten off yarn.

ch = chain, see page 18.

sl st = slip stitch, see page 19.

sc = single crochet, see page 20.

tr = treble crochet, see page 26.

cl = cluster, see page 46

Abbreviations and symbols, see page 180.

111

Sunflower lace

ch = chain,
see page 18.

sl st = slip stitch,
see page 19.

sc = single
crochet, see
page 20.

hdc = half
double crochet,
see page 22.

dc = double
crochet, see
page 24.

tr = treble
crochet, see
page 26.

Abbreviations
and symbols,
see page 180.

FOUNDATION RING: ch 4 and join with sl st to form a ring.

ROUND 1: ch 2 (counts as 1 sc), work 7 sc into ring, join with sl st to first ch of 2-ch.

ROUND 2: ch 4 (counts as 1 dc, ch 1), 1 dc into first sc, * ch 1, 1 dc into next sc; rep from * to end, ending last rep with ch 1, join with sl st into 3rd ch of 4-ch.

ROUND 3: ch 3 (counts as 1 dc), 3 dc into 1-ch-sp, * 1 dc into dc, 3 dc into ch-sp; rep from * to end, join with sl st into 3rd ch of 3-ch.

ROUND 4: ch 9 (counts as 1 tr, ch 5), 1 tr into same place as sl st, * skip 3 dc, [3 tr, ch 5, 3 tr] into next dc, skip 3 dc, [1 tr, ch 5, 1 tr] into next dc; rep from *, ending last rep with skip 3 dc, [3 tr, ch 5, 3 tr] into next dc, skip 3 dc, join with sl st into 4th ch of 9-ch.

ROUND 5: sl st over first 2 ch, 1 sc into 3rd ch, ch 7, * [3 tr, ch 5, 3 tr] into 5-ch-sp, ch 7, 1 sc into center of foll 5-ch-sp, ch 7; rep from *, ending last rep with [3 tr, ch 5, 3 tr] into 5-ch-sp, ch 7, join with sl st into first sc. Fasten off yarn.

111
📷↑

Spanish lace

🌀 **FOUNDATION RING:** ch 8 and join with sl st to form a ring.

ROUND 1: ch 2 (counts as 1 sc), work 15 sc into ring, join with sl st to 2nd ch of 2-ch.

ROUND 2: ch 5 (counts as 1 hdc, ch 3), * skip 1 sc, 1 hdc into next sc, ch 3; rep from * 6 times, join with sl st to 2nd ch of 5-ch.

ROUND 3: work [1 sc, 1 hdc, 3 dc, 1 hdc, 1 sc] into each ch-sp, join with sl st to first sc. (8 petals).

ROUND 4: ch 2, * ch 3, 1 sc into top of next petal, ch 6, 1 sc into top of next petal, ch 3, 1 hdc into sp before next sc at beg of next petal, ch 3, 1 hdc into same sp; rep from * twice, ch 3, 1 sc into top of next petal, ch 6, 1 sc into top of next petal, ch 3, 1 hdc into sp before sc at beg of next petal, ch 3, join with sl st to first ch of 3-ch.

ROUND 5: * ch 4, work [3 dc, ch 3, 3 dc] into 6-ch-sp, ch 4, 1 sc into hdc, 1 sc into 3-ch-sp, 1 sc into hdc; rep from * to end, join with sl st to first ch of 4-ch.

ROUND 6: * ch 5, 1 dc into each of next 3 dc, ch 5, insert hook into 3rd ch from hook and work 1 sc to make picot, ch 2, 1 dc into each of next 3 dc, ch 5, sl st into next sc, ch 4, insert hook into 3rd ch from hook and work 1 sc to make picot, ch 1, skip 1 sc, sl st into next sc; rep from * to end, join with sl st to first ch of 5-ch. Fasten off yarn.

ch = chain, see page 18.

sl st = slip stitch, see page 19.

sc = single crochet, see page 20.

hdc = half double crochet, see page 22.

dc = double crochet, see page 24.

tr = treble crochet, see page 26.

Abbreviations and symbols, see page 180.

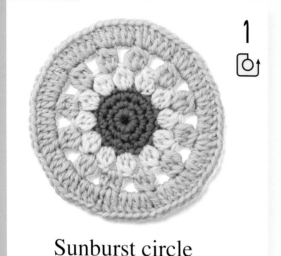

1

Sunburst circle

ch = chain,
see page 18.

sl st = slip stitch,
see page 19.

sc = single
crochet, see
page 20.

dc = double
crochet, see
page 24.

cl = cluster,
see page 46.

Abbreviations
and symbols,
see page 180.

Note

Worked in 3 colors, A, B,
and C.

✿ FOUNDATION RING: using yarn
A, ch 4 and join with sl st to form
a ring.

ROUND 1: ch 1, 6 sc into ring, join
with sl st into first sc.

ROUND 2: ch 1, [2 sc into next sc]
6 times, join with sl st into first sc.
(12 sc).

ROUND 3: ch 1, [2 sc into next sc]
12 times, join with sl st into
first sc. (24 sc).
Break off yarn A. Join yarn B to
any sc.

Special abbreviations

beg cl = beginning cluster
made from 2 dc sts.
cl = cluster made from
3 dc sts.

ROUND 4: ch 3 (counts as 1 dc),
beg cl into same sc, ch 2, skip
next sc, * cl into next sc, ch 2,
skip next sc; rep from * 10 times,
join with sl st into top of beg cl.
Break off yarn B. Join yarn C to
any 2-ch-sp.

ROUND 5: ch 3 (counts as 1 dc),
beg cl into same sp, ch 3, * cl into
next 2-ch-sp, ch 3; rep from *
10 times, join with sl st into top
of beg cl.

ROUND 6: ch 3, 2 dc into top of
beg cl, 3 dc into next 3-ch-sp,
*3 dc into top of next cl, 3 dc into
next 3-ch-sp; rep from * 10 times,
join with sl st into 3rd of 3-ch.
Fasten off yarn.

Wheel hexagon

◎ FOUNDATION RING: ch 6 and join with sl st to form a ring.
ROUND 1: ch 6 (counts as 1 tr, ch 2), 1 tr into ring, * ch 2, 1 tr into ring; rep from * 9 times, ch 2, join with sl st into 4th ch of 6-ch. (12 spaced tr).
ROUND 2: sl st into next 2-ch-sp, ch 3 (counts as 1 dc), [1 dc, ch 2, 2 dc] into same 2-ch-sp as sl st, * 3 dc into next 2-ch-sp, [2 dc, ch 2, 2 dc] into next 2-ch-sp; rep from * 4 times, 3 dc into next 2-ch-sp, join with sl st into 3rd ch of 3-ch.

ROUND 3: ch 3 (counts as 1 dc), 1 dc into next dc, [2 dc, ch 3, 2 dc] into ch-2 sp, 1 dc into each of next 7 dc, * [2 dc, ch 2, 2 dc] into next 2-ch-sp, 1 dc into each of next 7 dc; rep from * 4 times, ending last rep with 1 dc into each of next 5 dc, join with sl st into 3rd ch of 3-ch.
Fasten off yarn.

ch = chain, see page 18.

sl st = slip stitch, see page 19.

dc = double crochet, see page 24.

tr = treble crochet, see page 26.

Abbreviations and symbols, see page 180.

Note

Worked in 2 colors, A and B.

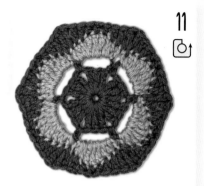

Flower hexagon

Spiral hexagon

ch = chain,
see page 18.

sl st = slip stitch,
see page 19.

sc = single
crochet, see
page 20.

hdc = half
double crochet,
see page 22.

dc = double
crochet, see
page 24.

tr = treble
crochet, see
page 26.

FOUNDATION RING: ch 4 and
join with sl st to form a ring.
ROUND 1: ch 7, 1 sc into ring,
[ch 6, 1 sc into ring] 5 times, sl st
in first ch of round.
ROUND 2: sl st in each of next 3 ch,
[ch 4, 1 sc in next 6-ch-loop]
6 times.
ROUND 3: [ch 4, 2 sc in next
4-ch-sp, 1 sc in next sc] 6 times.
ROUND 4: [ch 4, 2 sc in next
4-ch-sp, 1 sc in each of next 2 sc,
skip 1 sc] 6 times.
ROUND 5: [ch 4, 2 sc in next
4-ch-sp, 1 sc in each of next 3 sc,
skip 1 sc] 6 times.

FOUNDATION RING: using yarn
A, ch 6 and join with sl st to form
a ring.
ROUND 1 (RS): ch 4 (counts as
1 tr), 2 tr into ring, ch 1, *
3 tr into ring, ch 1; rep from *
4 times, join with sl st into 4th ch
of 4-ch, turn.
ROUND 2: * 1 sc into first 1-ch-sp,
ch 7; rep from * 5 times, join
with sl st into first sc, turn.
Break off yarn A. Join yarn B to
7-ch-lp.
ROUND 3: [1 hdc, 2 dc, 3 tr, 2 dc,
1 hdc] into each 7-ch-lp to make
petal, join with sl st into first hdc.
Break off yarn B.
Join yarn A to last hdc of petal.
ROUND 4: ch 4 (counts as 1 tr),
work 1 tr into each hdc, 1 dc into
each dc, 1 hdc into each tr made
on previous row, join with sl st
into 4th ch of 4-ch.
Fasten off yarn.

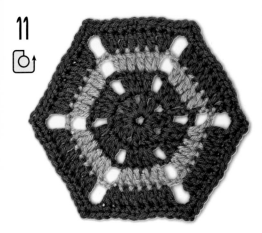

Striped hexagon

Note

Worked in 2 colors, A and B.

FOUNDATION RING: using yarn A, ch 6 and join with sl st to form a ring.

ROUND 1: ch 4 (counts as 1 dc, ch 1), [1 dc into ring, ch 1] 11 times, join with sl st into 3rd ch of 4-ch. (12 spaced dc).

ROUND 2: ch 3 (counts as 1 dc), 2 dc into 1-ch-sp, 1 dc into next dc, ch 2, * 1 dc into next dc, 2 dc into 1-ch-sp, 1 dc into next dc, ch 2; rep from * 4 times, join with sl st into 3rd ch of 3-ch. Break off yarn A. Join in yarn B.

ROUND 3: ch 3 (counts as 1 dc), 1 dc into same place, 1 dc into each of next 2 dc, 2 dc into next dc, ch 2, * 2 dc into next dc, 1 dc into each of next 2 dc, 2 dc into next dc, ch 2; rep from * 4 times, join with sl st into 3rd ch of 3-ch. Break off yarn B. Join in yarn A.

ROUND 4: ch 3 (counts as 1 dc), 1 dc into same place, 1 dc into each of next 4 dc, 2 dc into next dc, ch 2, * 2 dc into next dc, 1 dc into each of next 4 dc, 2 dc into next dc, ch 2; rep from * 4 times, join with sl st into 3rd ch of 3-ch.

ROUND 5: ch 1, 1 sc into same place, work 1 sc into each dc around hexagon and [2 sc, ch 1, 2 sc] into each 2-ch-sp, join with sl st into first sc.
Fasten off yarn.

ch = chain, see page 18.

sl st = slip stitch, see page 19.

sc = single crochet, see page 20.

dc = double crochet, see page 24.

Abbreviations and symbols, see page 180.

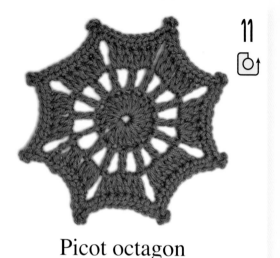

11

Picot octagon

ch = chain,
see page 18.

sl st = slip stitch,
see page 19.

sc = single
crochet, see
page 20.

dc = double
crochet, see
page 24.

cl = cluster,
see page 46.

Abbreviations
and symbols,
see page 180.

FOUNDATION RING: ch 8 and join with sl st to form a ring.

ROUND 1: ch 3 (counts as 1 dc), work 15 dc into ring, join with sl st into 3rd ch of 3-ch. (16 dc).

ROUND 2: ch 5 (counts as 1 dc, ch 2), [1 dc, ch 2] into each dc, join with sl st into 3rd ch of 3-ch. (16 spaced dc).

ROUND 3: cl st into next 2-ch-sp, ch 3 (counts as 1 dc), 2 dc into same 2-ch-sp, 3 dc into next 3-ch-sp, ch 3, [3 dc into next 2-ch-sp] twice, ch 3; rep from * 6 times, join with sl st into 3rd ch of 3-ch.

ROUND 4: ch 1, 1 sc into same place, 1 sc into each of next 5 dc, [2 sc, ch 3, 2 sc] into 3-ch-sp, * 1 sc into each of next 6 dc, [2 sc, ch 3, 2 sc] into 3-ch-sp; rep from * to end, join with sl st into first sc.
Fasten off yarn.

Two-color joining-square

Joining-square

Note

Worked in 2 colors, A and B.

FOUNDATION RING: using yarn A, ch 5 and join with sl st to form a ring.

ROUND 1: ch 3 (counts as 1 dc), work 15 dc into ring, join with sl st into 3rd ch of ch-3. (16 dc). Break off yarn A. Join in yarn B.

ROUND 2: ch 1, 1 sc into same place, 1 sc into each of next 3 dc, ch 2, [1 sc into each of next 4 dc, ch 2] 3 times, join with sl st into first sc.

ROUND 3: ch 1, 1 sc into same place, 1 sc into each of next 3 sc, 5 sc into 2-ch-sp, [1 sc into each of next 4 sc, 5 sc into 2-ch-sp] 3 times, join with sl st into first sc. Fasten off yarn.

FOUNDATION RING: ch 8 and join with sl st to form a ring.

ROUND 1: ch 3 (counts as 1 dc), work 15 dc into ring, join with sl st into 3rd ch of 3-ch. (16 dc).

ROUND 2: ch 1, 1 sc into same place, 1 sc into each of next 3 dc, ch 3, [1 sc into each of next 4 dc, 3 ch] 3 times, join with sl st into first sc.

ROUND 3: ch 1, 1 sc into same place, 1 sc into each of next 3 dc, [2 sc, ch 3, 2 sc] into 3-ch-sp, * 1 sc into each of next 4 dc, [2 sc, ch 3, 2 sc] into 3-ch-sp; rep from * twice, join with sl st into first sc. Fasten off yarn.

ch = chain, see page 18.

sl st = slip stitch, see page 19.

sc = single crochet, see page 20.

dc = double crochet, see page 24.

Abbreviations and symbols, see page 180.

Mallow

ch = chain,
see page 18.

sl st = slip
stitch, see
page 19.

sc = single
crochet, see
page 20.

hdc = half
double crochet,
see page 22.

dc = double
crochet, see
page 24.

Abbreviations
and symbols,
see page 180.

Note

Worked in 4 colors, A, B, C, and D.

Background block

🌀 **FOUNDATION CHAIN:** using yarn A, ch 29.

ROW 1 (RS): 1 sc into 2nd ch from hook, 1 sc into each ch to end, turn.

ROW 2: ch 1, 1 sc into each sc of previous row, turn.

Repeat row 2, 32 times more, ending with a WS row.

Fasten off yarn.

Flower motif

🌀 **FOUNDATION RING:** using yarn B, ch 4 and join with sl st into a ring.

ROUND 1: ch 5 (counts as 1 dc, ch 2), [1 dc into ring, ch 2] seven times, join with sl st into 3rd of 5-ch.

ROUND 2: sl st into next 2-ch-sp, ch 1, [1 sc, 1 hdc, 1 dc, 1 hdc, 1 sc] into same sp (petal made), [1 sc, 1 hdc, 1 dc, 1 hdc, 1 sc] into each rem ch sp, join with sl st into first sc.

Break off yarn B.

On the WS, join yarn C to one of the central spokes.

ROUND 3: using yarn C and working on the WS, ch 6 (counts as 1 dc, ch 3), [1 dc round next spoke, ch 3] seven times, join with sl st into 3rd of 6-ch.

ROUND 4: ch 1, turn flower to RS, working behind petals of round 2, [1 sc, ch 1, 5 dc, ch 1, 1 sc] into next 3-ch-sp (petal made), [1 sc, ch 1, 5 dc, ch 1, 1 sc] into each rem 3-ch-sp, join with sl st to first sc.

Fasten off yarn, leaving a long yarn tail.

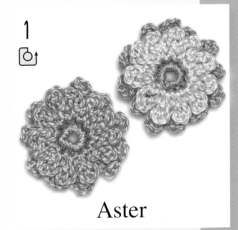

1

Aster

Leaf motifs (make 3)

🌀 **FOUNDATION CHAIN:** using yarn D and leaving a long yarn tail at the start, ch 11.

ROUND 1: working down one side of ch, 1 dc into 4th ch from hook, 1 dc into each of next 2 ch, 1 hdc into each of next 3 ch, 1 sc into next ch, 4 sc into last ch, working down other side of ch, 1 sc into next ch, 1 hdc into each of next 3 ch, 1 dc into each of next 2 ch, 2 dc into last ch.
Fasten off yarn and darn in this end.

After blocking, pin motifs to background block using photograph as a guide to placement. Stitch each motif in place with yarn tail, stitching down center of each leaf and between petals of flower.

Note

Worked in 2 colors, A and B.

🌀 **FOUNDATION RING:** using yarn A, ch 4 and join with sl st into a ring.

ROUND 1: ch 1, 11 sc into ring, change to B, 1 sl st in first ch of round. Do not cut A.

ROUND 2: Join B to same place, [1 sc, ch 4, 1 sc] in front loop of first ch of previous round, [1 sc, ch 4, 1 sc] in front loop of each sc, sl st in first sc of round.
Fasten off B. (12 small petals)

ROUND 3: Using A, work in empty back loops of round 1: [sl st, ch 7, 1 sc] in back loop of first ch, [1 sc, ch 7, 1 sc] in back loop of each sc, sl st in first sl st of round.
Fasten off. (12 large petals)

ch = chain, see page 18.

sl st = slip stitch, see page 19.

sc = single crochet, see page 20.

Abbreviations and symbols, see page 180.

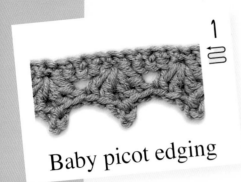

Baby picot edging

Shell braid

ch = chain,
see page 18.

sc = single
crochet, see
page 20.

dc = double
crochet, see
page 24.

cl = cluster, see
page 46.

Abbreviations
and symbols,
see page 180.

Special abbreviations

MP = make picot by working [ch 4, sl st into 4th ch from hook]

🌀 **FOUNDATION CHAIN:** multiple of 5 chains plus 5.
Make the required length of foundation chain.
ROW 1 (WS): 1 sc into 2nd ch from hook, 1 sc into each ch to end, turn.
ROW 2: ch 3, [1 dc, MP, 2 dc] into first sc, *skip next 4 sc, [2 dc, MP, 2 dc] into next sc; repeat from * to end.
Fasten off yarn.

🌀 **FOUNDATION CHAIN:** ch3
ROW 1 (RS): [3 dc, ch 3, 3 dc] into 3rd ch from hook, turn.
ROW 2: ch 3, [3 dc, ch 3, 3 dc] into 3-ch-sp of previous row, turn.
Repeat row 2 for length required.
Fasten off yarn.

⟐ **FOUNDATION CHAIN:** multiple of 4 chains plus 4.

Make the required length of foundation chain.

ROW 1 (RS): 1 sc into 2nd ch from hook, 1 sc into each ch to end, turn.

ROW 2: ch 1, 1 sc into first sc and into each sc to end, turn.

ROW 3: ch 1, 1 sc into first sc, *skip next sc, 5 dc into next sc, skip next sc, 1 sc into next sc; repeat from * to end.

Fasten off yarn.

Little shell edging

⟐ **FOUNDATION CHAIN:** multiple of 3 chains plus 3.

Thread beads onto B.

Using A, make the required length of foundation chain.

ROW 1: 1 sc into 6th ch from hook, *ch 2, skip 2 ch, 1 dc into the next ch; repeat from * to the end.

Fasten off. Join in B.

ROW 2: ch 3, into the next 2-ch-loop [1 dc, ch 1, place bead, ch 1, 2 dc] * into the next 2-ch-loop 2 dc, ch 1, place bead, ch 1, 2 dc; rep from * to end.

Fasten off yarn.

Beaded trim

Note

Worked in 2 colors, A and B.

ch = chain, see page 18.

sc = single crochet, see page 20.

dc = double crochet, see page 24.

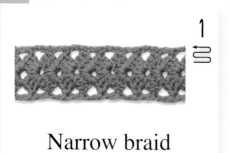

Narrow braid

1

⊙ FOUNDATION RING: ch 4 and join with sl st to form a ring.

ROW 1 (RS): ch 3 (counts as 1 dc), [3 dc, ch 2, 4 dc] into ring, turn.

ROW 2: ch 3, [3 dc, ch 2, 3 dc] into ch-2-sp, 1 dc into top of turning chain, turn.

Repeat row 2 for length required. Fasten off yarn.

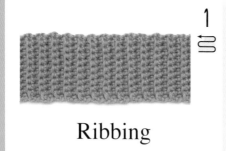

Ribbing

1

⊙ FOUNDATION CHAIN: ch 10. Make the required length of foundation chain.

ROW 1 (RS): 1 sc into 2nd ch from hook, 1 sc into each ch to end, turn.

ROW 2: ch 1, working into back loops only, 1 sc into each st along row, turn.

Rep row 2 for length required. Fasten off yarn.

ch = chain, see page 18.

sl st = slip stitch, see page 19.

sc = single crochet, see page 20.

dc = double crochet, see page 24.

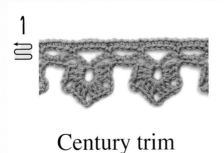

Century trim

🌀 **FOUNDATION CHAIN:** multiple of 11 chains plus 7.

Make the required length of foundation chain.

ROW 1 (RS): 1 sc into 2nd ch from hook, 1 sc into each ch to end, turn.

ROW 2: ch 1, 1 sc into first sc, ch 5, skip next 4 sc, 1 sc into next sc, *ch 9, sl st into 6th ch from hook, ch 3, skip next 5 sc, 1 sc into next sc, ch 5, skip next 4 sc, 1 sc into next sc; rep from * to end, turn.

ROW 3: ch 1, 2 sc into next ch-5-sp, *ch 1, [3 dc, ch 3] three times into next ch-6-sp, 3 dc into same ch-6-sp, ch 1, 2 sc into next ch-5-sp; repeat from * to end. Fasten off yarn.

Belgian lace

🌀 **FOUNDATION CHAIN:** ch 10.

ROW 1 (RS): 1 dc into 7th ch from hook, 1 dc into each ch to end, turn.

ROW 2: ch 6, 1 dc into each dc of previous row, turn.

Repeat row 2 for length required. Fasten off yarn.

ch = chain, see page 18.

sl st = slip stitch, see page 19.

sc = single crochet, see page 20.

dc = double crochet, see page 24.

Abbreviations and symbols, see page 180.

111 ⮋

Scallop edging

ch = chain,
see page 18.

sl st = slip stitch,
see page 19.

sc = single
crochet, see
page 20.

dc = double
crochet, see
page 24.

Abbreviations
and symbols,
see page 180.

🌀 **FOUNDATION CHAIN:** ch 5.
ROW 1 (WS): [3 dc, ch 3, 3 dc]
into 5th ch from hook, turn.
ROWS 2 & 3: ch 3, [3 dc, ch 3,
3 dc] into 3-ch-sp, turn.
ROW 4: ch 5, [3 dc, ch 3, 3 dc]
into 3-ch-sp, turn.
ROW 5 : ch 3, [3 dc, ch 3, 3 dc]
into 3-ch-sp, ch 2, [1 dc into
5-ch-sp, ch 2] five times,
[1 dc, 1 sc] into next 3-ch-sp,
turn, ch 3, 2 dc into next 2-ch-sp,
*sl st into next 2-ch-sp, ch 3, 2 dc
into same sp; repeat from * three
times, 1 sc into next 2-ch-sp, ch 3,
[3 dc, ch 3, 3 dc] into next
3-ch-sp, turn.
ROW 6: ch 3, [3 dc, ch 3, 3 dc]
into 3-ch-sp, turn.
ROW 7: ch 5, [3 dc, ch 3, 3 dc] into
3-ch-sp, turn.

Repeat rows 5–7 for length
required, ending with a row 4,
omitting instructions after
working 1 sc into 2-ch-sp.
Do not break yarn.
Turn edging so RS is facing,
scallops are along bottom edge
and beg working across top
of edging.
NEXT ROW: *ch 3, 3 sc into next
3-ch-sp; rep from * to end,
working last 3 sc into top of beg
5-ch, turn.
NEXT ROW: ch 1, 1 sc into each sc
of previous row, working 3 sc into
each 3-ch-sp, turn.
NEXT ROW: ch 1, 1 sc into each sc
of previous row.
Fasten off yarn.

Deep mesh edging

🌀 **FOUNDATION CHAIN:** ch 20.
ROW 1 (RS): 1 dc into 4th ch from hook, 1 dc into each of next 2 ch, *ch 1, skip next ch, 1 dc into next ch; repeat from * to end, turn.
ROW 2: ch 7, 1 dc into first dc, [ch 1, 1 dc into next dc] seven times, 1 dc into each of next 2 dc, 1 dc into 3rd of beg skipped 3-ch, turn.
ROW 3: ch 3, 1 dc into each of next 3 dc, *ch 1, 1 dc into next dc; repeat from * to end, turn.

ROW 4: ch 7, 1 dc into first dc, [ch 1, 1 dc into next dc] seven times, 1 dc into each of next 2 dc, 1 dc into 3rd of 3-ch, turn.
Repeat rows 3–4 for length required.
Fasten off yarn.

ch = chain, see page 18.

dc = double crochet, see page 24.

Abbreviations and symbols, see page 180.

174

Resources

Resources 175

Crochet hook specifications

Hooks from different manufacturers can vary widely in shape and size even though they may all be branded with the same number or letter. The material used to make the hook can also affect the gauge and effectively its working size.

Comparative steel crochet hook sizes (from smallest to largest)

For fine thread work steel crochet hooks tend to be used. It is possible to purchase tambour hooks used for chain stitch embroidery on a frame in sizes in between those given here. Tambour hooks tend not to have a thumb rest or handle and just have a smooth shank, which makes them slightly more difficult to use for crochet—ideal for tambour embroidery though.

Old UK	Metric (mm)	US
6	0.60	14
5$^1/_2$		13
5	0.75	12
4$^1/_2$		11
4	1.00	10
3$^1/_2$		9
3	1.25	8
2$^1/_2$	1.50	7
2	1.75	6
1$^1/_2$		5
1	2.00	4
1/0		3
2/0	2.50	2
3/0	3.00	1
0		0
00	3.50	00

US/metric equivalents

1 oz	=	28 g
1¾ oz	=	50 g
2 oz	=	57 g
3½ oz	=	100 g
1 in.	=	2.5 cm
4 in.	=	10 cm
1 yd	=	91.4 cm
39½ in.	=	1 m

Comparative aluminum and plastic crochet hook sizes (from smallest to largest)

Old UK	Metric (mm)	US
14	2	
13	2.25	B-1
12	2.5	
	2.75	C-2
11	3.00	
10	3.25	D-3
9	3.5	E-4
	3.75	F-5
8	4	G-6
7	4.5	7
6	5	H-8
5	5.5	I-9
4	6	J-10
3	6.5	K-10$^1/_2$
2	7	
0-1	8	L-11
00-000	9	M/N-13
	10	N/P-15
	15	P/Q
	16	Q
	19	S

The old English sizes have also been given because vintage hooks are still readily available and who knows what you might find on your travels. A word of warning though, old plastic hooks may become brittle, so do not use them on crochet work that will put a strain on the hook.

Useful hook and yarn combinations

Sport weight: B–E (2.5–3.5 mm)

Double knitting: E–G (3.5–4.5 mm)

Worsted weight: H–J (5–6 mm)

Yarn specifications

Yarns are available in a range of weights varying from very fine to very bulky. Although each weight of yarn is described by a specific name, there may actually be a lot of variation in the thicknesses when yarns are produced by different manufacturers or in different countries. The below reflect the most commonly used gauges and hook sizes for specific yarn categories.

Yarn weight category	Super fine	Fine	Light	Medium	Bulky	Super bulky
Type of yarns in category	Sock, fingering, baby	Sport, baby	DK, light worsted	Worsted, afghan, aran	Chunky	Bulky
Crochet gauge range in single crochet to 4 in. (10 cm)	23–32 sts	16–20 sts	12–17 sts	11–14 sts	8–11 sts	5–9 sts
Recommended hook in metric size range (mm)	2.25–3.5	3.5–4.5	4.5–5.5	5.5–6.5	6.5–9	9 and larger
Recommended hook US size range	B–1 to E–4	E–4 to 7	7 to I–9	I–9 to K–10½	K–10½ to M–13	M–13 and larger

Standard bed and blanket sizes

An afghan or blanket is always going to be a big project but here are a few measurements that will help you gain an understanding of what might be involved.

Bed	Mattress size	Quilt size*	Blocks (6 in. / 15 cm) square	Total number of blocks
Crib	23 × 46 in.	36 × 54 in.	6 × 9	54
	58 × 117 cm	90 × 135 cm		
Cot in UK	28 × 55 in.	36 × 60 in.	6 × 10	60
	70 × 140 cm	90 × 150 cm		
Buggy blanket		42–60 in. square	7–10 square	49–100
		105–150 cm square		
Single in UK	36 × 75 in.	48 × 84 in.	8 × 14	112
	90 × 190 cm	120 × 210 cm		
Twin	39 × 75 in.	54 × 84 in.	9 × 14	126
	99 × 190 cm	135 × 210 cm		
Double	54 × 75 in.	66 × 84 in.	11 × 14	154
	135 × 190 cm	165 × 210 cm		
Queen US (King in UK)	60 × 80 in.	72 × 90 in.	12 × 15	180
	150 × 200 cm	180 × 225 cm		
Super King in UK	72 × 80 in.	84 × 90 in.	14 × 15	210
	180 × 200 cm	210 × 225 cm		
King in US	76 × 80 in.	90 × 90 in.	15 × 15	225
	193 × 200 cm	225 × 225 cm		

* Mattress size plus a 6 in. (15 cm) overhang on three sides. This number has been made to be divisible by whole 6 in. (15 cm) square blocks.

Abbreviations and symbols

Not all the following are used in this book but it is always useful to have a comprehensive list.

1   Easy
11   Intermediate
111   Experienced

⟨◍⟩   Worked in rounds
≋   Worked in rows

ABCD   Yarn colors
alt   Alternate
bl   Back loop: yarn over hook as indicated by stitch, hook is inserted through the back loop only as it is presented at the point of working the st indicated.
bp   Back post: yarn over hook as indicated by stitch, insert the hook from the back through to the front and back to the back, round the post of the st indicated and complete the st indicated.
beg   Beginning
cont   Continue
foll   Follow(ing)
fl   Front loop: hook is inserted through the front loop only as it is presented at the point of working the stitch indicated.

fp   Front post: yarn over hook as indicated by stitch, insert the hook from the front through to the back and back to the front round the post of the stitch indicated, and complete the stitch indicated.
lp(s)   Loop(s)
mb   Make bobble: a group of stitches worked into the same space or st and worked to the point before the last yarn over hook to complete the stitches and joined with a yarn over hook loop drawn through all the stitches, as instructed in the pattern.
patt   Pattern
pb   Place bead, as instructed in pattern.
rep   Repeat
rev sc   Reverse single crochet (crab stitch): working from left to right, insert the hook into the st or space indicated, yarn over hook, pull loop.
rnd   Round
RS   Right side: the side of the work on display.
sk   Skip
sp   Space
st (s)   Stitches
tog   Together
WS   Wrong side: the side of the work not seen.
yo   Yarn over hook

*		Start of repeat
[]		Repeat the instruction within the brackets the stated number of times.
▲		Starting point
←		Direction of working
△		Join in new yarn
▲		Fasten off yarn: cut yarn 4 in. (10 cm) from the hook and draw the yarn through the loop.
⌒	bl	Back loop: work the st indicated through the top, back, loop only of the st as presented at the point of working the st indicated.
⌣	fl	Front loop: work the st indicated through the top, front, loop only of the st as presented at the point of working the st indicated.
•	sl st	Slip stitch: insert the hook into the st or sp indicated, yo, pull lp through st and the lp on the hook.
✶	sl stbl	Slip stitch through the back loop: insert the hook into the bl st indicated, yo, pull lp through st and the lp on the hook.
○	ch	Chain: yo and draw through lp or slip knot on the hook.
+ †	sc	Single crochet: insert the hook into the st or sp indicated, yo, pull lp through st, yo, draw lp through the 2 lps on the hook.
⊼	scbl	Single crochet through the back loop only (see bl opposite).
⊥	scfl	Single crochet through the front loop only (see fl opposite).
⋏	sc2tog	Single crochet together: work two single crochet sts into the sp or st indicated to the point of the final yo and the completion of the stitch, yo and draw the yarn through both sts to complete them.
	sc3tog	Single crochet together 3 sts, as for 2 sts for sc2tog.
T	hdc	Half double crochet: yo, insert the hook into the st or sp indicated, yo, pull lp through st, yo, draw lp through all the lps on the hook.
Ŧ	dc	Double crochet: yo, insert the hook into the st or sp indicated, yo, pull loop through st, yo, draw lp through 2 lps on the hook, yo, draw yarn through the last 2 lps on the hook.
Ⱦ	dcbl	Double crochet through the back loop only (see bl opposite).
Ŧ	dcfl	Double crochet through the front loop only: (see fl opposite).
Ŧ	dcbp/ bpdc	Double crochet round the back post (see bp left).
Ŧ	dcfp/ fpdc	Double crochet round the front post (see fp left).

dcfpst   Double crochet round the front post of the last st worked (see fp on page 180).

dtr   Double treble crochet: yo 3 times, insert the hook into the st or sp indicated, yo, pull lp through st, then rep yo, draw lp through 2 lps on the hook until only 1 lp remains on the hook.

dc2tog   Double crochet together: work two double crochet sts into the sp or st indicated to the point of the final yo and the completion of the stitch, yo and draw the yarn through both sts to complete them.

dc3tog   Double crochet together 3 sts, as for 2 sts for dc2tog.

tr   Treble crochet: yo twice, insert the hook into the st or sp indicated, yo, pull loop through st, then rep yo, draw lp through 2 lps on the hook until only 1 lp remains on the hook.

trbp/ bptr   Treble crochet round the back post (see bp on page 180).

trfp/ fptr   Treble crochet round the front post (see fp on page 180).

tr2tog   Treble crochet together: work two treble crochet sts into the sp or st indicated to the point of the final yo and the completion of the stitch, yo and draw the yarn through both sts to complete them.

tr3tog   Treble crochet together 3 sts, as for 2 sts for tr2tog.

pb   Place bead: slide bead along yarn to the base of the hook or as indicated in patt.

pb   Place bead: slide bead along yarn to the base of the hook before the ch st indicated.

pb   Place bead: remove the hook and slide the bead along the yarn, insert the hook through the bead from the opposite side from the ch lp. Hook the ch lp and draw through the bead. Pass the bead onto the ch of sts before working the last yo.

cl   Cluster: a group of sts worked to the point before the last yo to complete the st and joined with a yo lp drawn through all the sts.

	mcl	Make cluster: ch 2 st, 2dc sts in the sp below the base of the chain-2 and between the last 2 dc sts worked to the point of the final yo, yo draw yarn through all the lps on the hook.
	ps	Puff or bobble stitch: a group of sts that meet at the top and the bottom; worked to the point before the last yo to complete the st and joined with a yo lp drawn through all the stitches. Note the appearance of the top of the group of stitches.
	ml	Make loop: lp the yarn around the middle finger of the left hand, insert the hook into the st indicated, draw both strands of yarn at the base of the lp through the st, and complete the st indicated. Tighten the lp by pulling the two parts of the lp in opposite directions.
□	**om**	Open mesh in filet crochet: ch 1, sk 1 sp or dc st, dc into the next dc st or as indicated in patt.
■	**sm**	Solid mesh in filet crochet: dc into the next sp or st, dc into the next dc st or as indicated in patt.
		Broomstick crochet stitch: working from left to right, insert the hook into the st indicated, yo, draw the yarn through, and place the lp onto the knitting needle or strip of card.
—		Surface crochet: as indicated in pattern.

Equivalent stitch names
The stitch names for some of the sts differ in the different areas of the world. Even more confusingly, the same names are used but they describe a different stitch.

American	**English**
single crochet	double crochet
half double crochet	half treble crochet
double crochet	treble crochet
treble crochet	double treble crochet
double treble crochet	triple treble crochet

Glossary

Ball band
The paper strip or paper tag on a ball or skein of yarn. A ball band gives information about weight, shade number, dye lot number, and fiber content of the yarn. It may also show care instructions and other details, including yardage and suggested gauge and hook size.

Blocking
Setting a piece of crochet by stretching and pinning it out on a flat surface before steaming or treating with cold water.

Bobble
Several stitches worked in the same place and joined together at the top to make a decorative raised bump. Bobbles are often worked on a background of shorter stitches.

Border
A deep, decorative strip of crochet, usually worked with one straight and one shaped edge that is used for trimming pieces of crochet or fabric.

Braid
A narrow, decorative strip of crochet similar in appearance to a purchased furnishing braid.

Broomstick crochet
A particular type of crochet, worked with both a crochet hook and a "broomstick" such as a large knitting needle.

Chain space
Space formed by working lengths of chain stitches between other stitches. Also known as chain loops or chain arches.

Cluster
Several incomplete stitches worked together so they join at the top.

Decrease
Removing one or more stitches to reduce the number of working stitches.

Dye lot
The batch of dye used for a specific ball of yarn. Shades can vary between batches, so always use yarn from the same dye lot to make an item.

Edge finish
A decorative crochet edging worked directly into the edge of a piece of crochet.

Edging
A narrow strip of crochet, usually with one straight and one shaped edge, used for trimming pieces of crochet or fabric.

Fan

Several stitches worked into the same chain or stitch but not joined at the top which make a fan, or shell.

Fiber

Natural or man-made substances spun together to make yarn.

Filet crochet

Filet crochet patterns are worked solidly and set against a regularly worked mesh background. Filet crochet is usually worked from a graphic chart rather than written instructions.

Foundation chain

A length of chain stitches that forms the base for a piece of crochet.

Foundation row

In a stitch pattern, the first row worked into the foundation chain. The foundation row is not repeated as part of the pattern.

Gauge

The looseness or tightness of a crochet fabric expressed as a specific number of rows and stitches in a given area, usually 4 in. (10 cm) square.

Heading

Extra rows of plain crochet worked on the long straight edge of an edging or border to add strength and durability.

Increase

Adding one or more stitches to increase the number of working stitches.

Intarsia

Intarsia produces a design featuring areas of different colors which are each worked with a separate small ball of yarn. Intarsia patterns are worked in two or more colors from a colored chart on a grid. Each colored square on the chart represents one stitch.

Jacquard

Jacquard patterns are similar to intarsia, but the yarns are continued along the row rather than being used separately. A Jacquard pattern is shown as a colored chart on a grid. Each colored square on the chart represents one stitch.

Lace

A stitch pattern forming an openwork design similar in appearance to lace fabric.

Mesh

A stitch pattern forming a regular geometric grid.

Motif

A shaped piece of crochet, often worked in rounds. Several motifs can be joined together rather like fabric patchwork to make a larger piece. Also known as a medallion or block.

Pattern

A set of instructions showing exactly how to make a garment or other crochet item.

Pattern repeat
The number of rows or rounds that are needed to complete one stitch pattern.

Picot
A decorative chain space often closed into a ring with a slip stitch. The number of chains in a picot can vary.

Ply
A single strand of yarn made by twisting fibers together. Most yarn is made from two or more plies twisted together to make different yarn weights, although some woolen yarns are made from a single thick ply.

Puff
A cluster of three or more half double crochet stitches worked into the same place, and joined together at the top to make a raised stitch.

Right side
The front of crochet fabric. This side is usually visible on a finished item, although some stitch patterns may be reversible.

Round
A row of crochet stitches worked in the round; the last stitch of one round is joined to the first stitch of the same round. Rounds of crochet can form flat motifs or tubular shapes.

Row
A line of stitches worked from side to side to make a flat piece of crochet.

Seam
The join made where two edges are stitched or crocheted together.

Sewing needle
A needle with a sharp point used for applying a crochet braid, edging, or border to a piece of fabric.

Spike
A decorative stitch worked by inserting the hook from front to back of the work, one or more rows below the normal position, and/or to the right or left of the working stitch.

Starting chain
A specific number of chain stitches worked at the beginning of a round to bring the hook up to the correct height for the next stitch that is being worked.

Stitch pattern
A sequence or combination of crochet stitches that is repeated over and over again to create a piece of crochet fabric.

Surface crochet
Rows of decorative crochet worked on top of a crochet background.

Symbol chart
Charts that describe a crochet pattern visually, by using symbols to indicate the different stitches and exactly where and how they should be placed in relation to one another.

Tapestry needle
A large, blunt-ended embroidery needle used for seaming pieces of crochet together. May be curved or straight.

Trim
A length of crochet worked separately and sewn to a main piece, or onto plain fabric, as a decoration.

Tunisian crochet
A particular type of crochet worked with a special long hook. Tunisian crochet is worked back and forth in rows without turning the work.

Turning chain
A specific number of chain stitches worked at the beginning of a row to bring the hook up to the correct height for the next stitch that is being worked.

Wrong side
The reverse side of crochet fabric; this side is not usually visible on a finished item.

Yarn needle
A very large blunt-pointed needle used for sewing pieces of crochet together..

Index

Acknowledgments

All photographs and illustrations are the copyright of Quarto Inc. While every effort has been made to credit contributors, Quarto would like to apologize should there have been any omissions or errors—and would be pleased to make the appropriate correction for future editions of the book.

Some of the material in this book first appeared in:
The Crochet Stitch Bible by Betty Barnden
200 Crochet Blocks by Jan Eaton
200 Crochet Techniques by Jan Eaton
200 Ripple Stitch Patterns by Jan Eaton
200 Stitch Patterns for Baby Blankets by Jan Eaton
Crochet Basics by Jan Eaton
The Encyclopedia of Crochet Techniques by Jan Eaton